STEVEN MAST

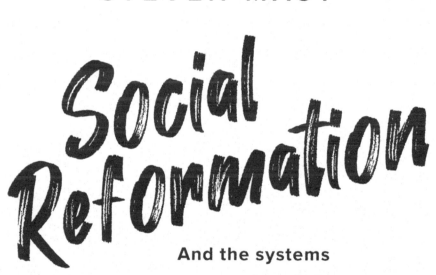

Social
Reformation

And the systems
that define us

Social Reformation

And the systems that define us.

© 2022 Steven Mast

Print ISBN: 978-1-66784-084-0
eBook ISBN: 978-1-66784-085-7

INTRO

THIS INTRO MAY SERVE AS more of a disclaimer than anything. I do not intend to attack anyone's beliefs or offend anyone. I do not pretend to know everything. My intent is not so much to give answers to problems but rather to spark thought outside the box of current society, systems and structures. I want to challenge the normal thoughts and ideas when it comes to culture and religion. I also want people to know that I do not "white knuckle" my beliefs. I realize that I could be wrong and try not to make too many absolute statements. I also don't have a problem if others don't agree with me or see eye to eye on certain issues. Not agreeing is OK. There is nothing wrong with that. I try not to set many posts because my beliefs have and most likely will change over time. Having too many absolutes is how I become too rigid and stagnant, because then I tend to believe all must believe the way that I do. This causes me to always be stuck trying to defend my positions rather than engaging in constructive dialogue with others. I am guilty of this myself. I all too often found identity in my beliefs and chose to defend those over other people. I believe that healthy views and opinions are ones that have been challenged and thoughtfully worked through. This normally causes us to truly hear opposing views and to realize there are many different world views outside of our own. Absolutes become the very things that do not allow one to progress. I believe that hard-nosed stances are the very things that have hindered the growth of humanity for ions. I am fairly certain on a few points that some may find hard to move past. I am fairly certain that most of the major religions have "white knuckled their beliefs" and have hindered the progressive development of society. I believe nationalism coupled with religion are responsible for the greatest evils ever committed. I do not see any way around taking torture and evil in the human realm and calling it love in the divine realm. I realize this is a very touchy subject and I want to navigate it as such. I do not wish to make anyone feel attacked or marginalized. I come from a Western culture and a Western Christian religion and as such I use these as my points of reference throughout the book. I do however realize that there are many nations and religions that suffer similar issues or problems. I do not wish to stir up anger and resentment and if that is what the reading of this book will do then feel free to discontinue reading at any time. If, however you can put disagreements to the side and move on then please continue reading. Sometimes taking in contrary opinions is best done one small "bite" at a time. Read a little and chew on it a bit, then read some more.

I also want to make clear that the critique of different systems is just that. It is a critique or maybe criticism of systems, not people. I feel that many people caught up in upholding faulty social systems are victims of these systems as well. Normally when someone acts or perpetuates beliefs that are unbecoming of their true identities, in my opinion, it usually comes from an outside influence such as an established social system. When I mention the police, military, nations, religions, and so on, I am talking of some policies or beliefs that influence these institutions, not the whole organization and most certainly not the individuals. There is a big difference between criticizing systems that influence our society and criticizing individual people.

I will also mention that I do not use a lot of citations in this book for a couple of reasons. The first is that anyone can do research and "find evidence" to back up whatever beliefs they want. If someone sees a citation and takes the information as fact based on that citation alone, then that is essentially perpetuating the problems that I address in the book. It is once again just taking someone's word for it without checking it yourself. My goal in this book is to create thought and interest. If a subject catches your eye and you wish to know more about it, then my aim is to cause you to investigate it yourself without me giving you a prescribed set of resources. It gives you the opportunity to see multiple sides of any issue without me feeding you resources that only back up my opinions. You can quite literally justify any opinion through "research", and quite honestly, the word has been so misused that I immediately question the research someone claims they did. It builds zero trust in me when the average joe claims they "researched" something. If I was writing on one subject and attempting to make a deep dive into any one thing in particular, then I should definitely have citations, but that simply is not this book.

I will mention in closing, when I find my identity through systems and establishments, it is very easy to become offended when these systems are criticized. I can attach myself to anything, so being offended is easy when these systems are challenged. It is important to realize that our identity should never be derived from manmade systems and structures. To do this cuts us short of our true value and abilities. You are way bigger and better than anything human have ever created.

CHAPTER 1:

WHAT DOES THIS ALL MEAN?

As I SIT TO WRITE this book, I am not writing from a place of composure or being "put together" by any stretch of the imagination. I am actually writing from a place of uncertainty, asking myself the same questions I present in this book. This is more of an insight into my own questioning than anything else. I can't help but wonder if we, our planet, solar system, galaxy and even universe are floating around on a speck more consistent with "Whoville" than anything else, with an alternate realm of existence just outside of our observation. What if we, and all that is around us, are part of a much larger entity, the same way that we are comprised of protons, electrons, atoms, strands of DNA and cells? What if our universe and the galaxies therein are of similar content, building something much larger and beyond our imagination? What if a galaxy is merely a cell among trillions of others that comprises something much bigger? We humans being much the same, could we be building blocks to something much bigger? Could we humans be much like an atom in a cell, floating through existence on a speck and unaware of the expanse of existence beyond what is us. Are the cells within our bodies and within all that exists, their own galaxy or even their own universe? Where does it all begin? Where does it end? Are we as humans merely in a progression between the beginning and the end? Does it even end? Is it as broad, or as narrow, as what our imaginations are willing to create? Does the universe only stop at the end of our imagination? The possibilities are so vast, and the frontiers of wonder are so great, yet we are here, on this earth fighting over who becomes our next president. The universe, so pliable and willing to conform to our immense desires and imaginations, stands still as we fight for better fuel prices. Humanity sits, bickers, and divides on the subject of climate change and what is causing it, not realizing we could all be wrong. We could all be right at the same time, containing an element of truth in us all. What if climate change goes beyond carbon emissions and greenhouse gasses? Could the earth and all of existence be linked into us, into who we are? Could quantum entanglement go far beyond our imagination. Could we be the energy from which all else finds its pulse? We find humanity progressively spiraling into disarray, and somehow our climate is doing the same thing. It seems recently we see more hurricanes, tornados, floods, drought, fire, and just overall crazy weather patterns. We have had a lot of new sickness and even a pandemic over the last couple of decades. Humanity is going through a huge upheaval right now. Could we be creating it all? Could the upheaval be the immune system of the universe, fighting back at all that plagues it? Could we be holding onto the very things that the universe is attempting to rid itself from? Can we likewise be the power of restoration? The scale of our upheaval is probably bigger than it has ever been. Could the universe simply be mirroring back to us the state of disarray that humanity finds itself in? As dark as it all may feel at the moment, could our outlook be equally as bright? I feel the heaviness, I feel the darkness, but I also see the possibility of light as we have never seen before. I need the sunlight. If I sit indoors for too long, my body cries for sunshine. Can we, as the creators of the darkness around us, equally be the bearers of the very light we so desperately need? Could both the darkness and the light be something that is contained within us? In an attempt to reach a place where the light can be attained, a walk through our darkness may be required. Only when we realize that the darkness around us is the creation of our own social constructs, can we as the creators of this darkness begin to bring in the light.

We as a human species are more destructive and lethal than ever, but could we be just as loving and nurturing? The twentieth century has been the bloodiest century in history with the number of dead attributed to war alone being estimated at around 187 million people. Could nature be feeling this stress and darkness that we are manifesting? Could our tumultuous existence be the reason for nature's upheaval as well? In other words, could the universe be manifesting the energies that we are projecting out into it? Maybe humans are powerful enough that nature tends to follow us in some mimetic way. What if all of nature including the earth and our weather, animals, and us all come together as one living organism? Could the earth be alive, and we just have such a narrow vision of "life" that we are totally missing the definition? Is the whole universe a living breathing thing, and we are just a small part of it all? If we molest this earth for our own gain without consideration of how we are hurting our planet, then how long will it let us continue without pushing back? Will the rest of creation resist humanity and our destructiveness until we are gone? Will it continue to ramp up its resistance to us, the same way our bodies fight any disease? There is already a study and theory of our continued molestation of the planet releasing more new diseases the farther we invade and violate nature. Nature's built in immune system perhaps? When a bear, cougar, or buffalo attacks a human on a hiking trail, we tend to call them dangerous. We will normally pursue and kill the attacking animal as something purely evil. We pretend to not understand why these animals would do such a thing. Sure there could be animals with evil intent similar to humans, but we normally do not consider the fact that we humans are the most dangerous creature on the planet. We kill way more animals in a single hunting season than the number of humans killed by all the animals combined. Could even the animals be fighting back to some degree? Do they know, even if it is through a different form of consciousness, how dangerous and harmful we are? If I was them, I'd keep my kids away from us too. Almost everything else around us, from the large to the small, from plants to animals, are all participating together, in harmony to nurture this earth and their ecosystems. We humans, the most "developed" animals of us all seem to be the only ones fighting for our right to destroy it. We, rather than living with creation seek to dominate it. Do we have a misconception of what a developed and conscious creature is? Maybe we have a stronger or more powerful brain in some way, but maybe it's just different and not so much better. If we shift our perspective of intelligence we could see that being able to build things does not necessarily mean that we are more intelligent. A dog often seems to be much happier than humans. If the ability to have inner peace, or to feel joy and love were the measuring rods for intelligence, then maybe our pet's intelligence could almost be seen as higher than ours. I don't know. It just seems to me that for all the intelligence we claim to have, we can do some really dumb stuff.

What about our understanding of civilization and what it really means to be civilized? Who gave the definition of what civilized means? Was it a European person sitting in a nice house with four walls and a cozy fireplace? Why did we feel the need to define it? Was it another tool by which we sought superiority to justify our quest to subjugate the "less civilized?" Was it another tool used to label and isolate those living in the land that we wished to acquire? Should civilization be defined by our technology and the things we possess, or by how we treat each other? Shouldn't our actions be a display of how civilized we are rather than our ability to produce a smart phone? The way people conquered and subjugated other people groups reveals the barbaric and savage nature of the conquerors, not the ones they subjugated. Who was to say that the tribal cultures of Africa, Australia, Asia, the Americas were not civilized? Why were they viewed as barbaric and savage? The conquest of the Americas and the enslavement of Africans revealed more about our level of being civilized (or lack there of), rather than the other way around. The tribal people around the globe seemed to be thriving just fine and generally seemed to have life more figured out. They seemed to be living as part of their ecosystems and in harmony with the rest of nature for the most part. The settlement and conquest of many of these lands destroyed most of that. European "civilization" tended to be the downfall of most of the continents they inhabited. Pestilence, war, and famine seemed to go wherever "civilization" went. The loss of life went wherever "civilization" went. The disease, famine, and war took so many lives of native tribal cultures across the globe that it is impossible to even estimate the numbers in any constructive way. European conquest and civilization seemed to spread more like a viscous cancer than anything else. Maybe our version of civilization is more like the polar opposite of what it should be. Why do we even need to define it anyway? Maybe through conquest and settlement we have turned humanity into the virus of the universe. Maybe the universe is coming together, like any known living thing, and is fighting to rid itself of the virus that is killing it. I do tend to believe that we humans are much more powerful than we could ever dream of. Our power can destroy (which seems to be what we are focused on right now), or we can be life givers and heal this place just as easily. We can also bring life to the universe in a very beautiful way, but we cannot do it under our current mentality, structures, and systems.

The possibilities of imagination are so great and yet we find ourselves here, fighting over the most trivial things in comparison to it all. Imagination can do just as much real work as a general laborer building a new home. We tend to focus on the material things that we can physically discern. The things we physically see and touch do not necessarily give us a complete view of reality. Some believe that the unseen universe is every bit as real as the observable universe. Some humans wish to explore vast unseen realms, and others see no reality outside of their physical senses. There is a portion of humanity that wants to know what is beyond the stars, and a portion who cares only about their nation or religion, and nothing else. Part of humanity envisions an existence so vast that it defies human reasoning, others just want cheaper gas at the pumps. This is not meant to ridicule or belittle anyone. I simply think it is time for humanity to take the lids off our imaginations and reconsider what is important and real. My inner self just knows that mankind as a whole is not living up to our full potential, not even close actually. Are new possibilities literally unlocked through our curiosity and our willingness to explore these possibilities? Can we literally create things that did not exist before, simply through our imagination and the pursuit of the unknown? What if through our exploration and sense of wonderment, there is something else out there that hears us crying out? I fully believe that humanity has no idea what we are a part of or what the possibilities are. I do not profess to have answers to much of anything that I am writing about. My goal is not to have answers but rather to inspire thought. I would like to push my own imagination to the limit, but I first need to process the "here and now". I first need to understand the world I live in and attempt to throw out the things that don't matter. I first need to recognize the reality that we humans have created, but not necessarily the reality that must exist. I believe we all as a species need to look around us and differentiate between what is there because it is essential, and what is there because it has always been there, what we created. I believe that somehow humanity needs to broaden our vision of exploration. We can explore thought, ideas, and imagination the same way that we explore the oceans. We do not need to stop exploring the planet or space. We need to further explore everything that is around us, but maybe we also need to explore ideas and thought in a way we are not used to. Even our imaginations are held captive to the constructs of society, government, and religion that humanity has built. I love the idea of once again placing a human on the moon. I love our exploration of Mars and our attempts to see into the far reaches of the universe. I love our human drive to climb the tallest mountains and dive to the lowest seas, but we can't stop there. A famous mountaineer of the early twentieth century George Mallory summed up the human drive and passion for exploration in a very beautiful way. Mount Everest had never been climbed at this point in history and some people thought him, and the expedition he was part of, were crazy for attempting to summit the mountain. There was actually great controversy on whether such an "unnecessary" thing should be done. Afterall, what would this accomplish? What good would come from such an accomplishment? George Mallory was part of a previous expedition attempting to summit Mount Everest and it resulted in seven men losing their lives. Despite all this he was joining another expedition in preparation to give it another attempt. When he was asked "Why did you want to climb Mount Everest?" he responded with the famous phrase "Because it's there". What a beautiful response! I believe that those words sum things up beautifully for humanity's drive to push the limits of possibility. This drive is an absolute necessity for the advancement of mankind and should never be snuffed out in any way. We need this drive. It is absolutely vital for our future. Mallory ended up dying in his attempt to climb Mount Everest in 1924. We can ask whether his attempts were worth anything if he never accomplished his goals. He never summited Everest and ended up dying trying to accomplish it. Throughout history people have debated regulating expeditions such as this due to its danger. Many mountaineers both male and female have perished in their attempts of reaching the tops of mountains. One could argue that Mallory died in vain and that it was a waste of a good human life. One could argue that viewpoint very well, however there are many things to consider.

From the most basic viewpoint, climbers who superseded Mallory could use the route he chose and take it a bit further due to his exploration of that particular route. His exploration led the way for many people to summit the mountain. Humans were wondering if a person could actually reach those heights and survive. This was an unknown elevation realm for humanity, and he helped push our understanding of it. For Mallory himself it would have most likely been an equally fatal blow to him as a person if another person or committee would have stepped in and prevented him from attempting it. It would have taken the dream and the spark out of his life, and he would have probably gone to the grave as an unhappy and defeated man. A person with such visions, drive and determination must be allowed to pursue their dreams and visions because the inability to pursue may prove to be just as fatal as the pursuit. I think this may be the cause of much of the depression and anxiety that runs rampant in our society. People can easily turn to much more foolish endeavors such as alcohol and drugs that can kill a person just as quickly as a dangerous expedition. To withhold such lofty goals from a driven human serves to be just as destructive to the human's emotional state as a physical neutering would be to that person. A person becomes so unmotivated and depressed that one could argue that the physical death of a person who is whole heartedly in pursuit of their goals would be much more humane. Another factor to take into consideration is that people such as Mallory keep the spirit of exploration alive within humanity. I believe it is literally as much a part of our evolutionary DNA as any other part of our anatomy. If we as a species snuff out the spirit and drive of exploration, then it, in my opinion would be removed from our species the same way that a physical feature can be phased out of a creature that no longer needs it. There are sea creatures who still have minor bones of appendages such as legs inside their bodies. These appendages became useless to them, so nature began "phasing them out", yet there are still remnants that remain. I believe certain character attributes in a species can be phased out in much the same way. Since we as a human race depend so heavily on the spirit of adventure, I believe that if adventure were to disappear from our species it would ultimately lead to the destruction of us all. We rely heavily on the spirit of adventure and exploration to move us forward in the search for new and better things. Explorers both past and present, both male and female literally keep the quest for advancement alive within our species. They keep drive, motivation, and ingenuity coursing through our veins. It is my belief that anything that becomes stagnant, unable, or unwilling to continue to advance becomes obsolete and will ultimately be taken out of existence, therefore it is imperative that we as a human race continue to push forward and advance.

The place that humanity finds itself at right now is of paramount importance. I feel as though we have become stagnant on several different levels. I believe we have reached a point of stagnation in several areas of our progressive development. We continue to advance and explore technology, science, geography, and general learning, yet somehow we have become stagnant in the development of our culture and society as a species. At the very least, our progression in cultural society has become greatly arrested. We continue to follow the same direction and structures of society such as economics and religion that have been in place for thousands of years. In society we have gone through many different types of government, yet even though they may have been relabeled, the basic premise remains the same. We have had monarchies, republics, democracies, communism, socialism, capitalism, feudal systems, and the list goes on, however the basic premise of a person devoting their life to a job every day, wasting their life away in support of some other entity or person remains the same. We fight so hard to hold up our systems to appear superior to the "others". We undergo this agony because we believe it is the only way to provide for our families. We sacrifice our goals, dreams, and families in the pursuit of this lifestyle because it has always been done this way. We have been taught that this is the only way. This lifestyle has produced more depressed, unmotivated, and just generally unhappy people than we will ever know. It is probably impossible to estimate the number of lives that this depressing existence has taken, and for what?

We still have major governments competing with each other, sending their young people to war and killing so many other humans for such trivial things! We continue to participate in the barbaric notion that we should strive to move our nation and the people within its borders forward at all costs. We often do this at the expense of other nations rather than attempting to unite as a species, to propel us forward as a single unit. We still depend on local economies and their up and down cycles, bringing prosperity to some, and a life of destitution to others. As a result, I can live fat and healthy as a middleclass citizen in America while people on the same planet starve to death because they have no money for food. The system that also does not allow for the necessities of life because one does not have the money for it, is a barbaric system as well. We have progressed in the sense that it has generally become unacceptable to conquer other nations and humans for the sole purpose of gaining more land, however we just find other things to fight over. You can see this (regardless of political stance or opinions) in the hugely unpopular war in Ukraine. People don't so much care who is at fault, they just want it to stop. We as Americans no longer kill others for their land per se, but we will kill you for the resources that your land contains. We can no longer conquer you to outright enslave your people, but we will kill you for not producing and giving us what we want at the price we demand. We will paint you in an evil way through a publicity program in order to gain the popular opinion that violent action is required. We haven't progressed at all when it comes to war and the killing of others, we have just relabeled it to whatever sounds more acceptable at the time. China for example still targets the Uyghurs and others in Xinjiang to the point of being labeled as a genocide. They get away with it by labeling it as being part of the "war on terror" yet the real reasons lie much deeper. If it is no longer acceptable to conquer a land for its diamonds or oil, we will instead demonize in whatever way necessary the peoples of that land in order to make war and the killing of others more palatable. It is still in large for the same thing, and with the same end result, it has only been relabeled as something else.

When it comes to religion, we have done much of the same. We haven't really progressed, we have merely relabeled some things. From the religions of ancient societies such as the Egyptians, Greeks and Romans to the modern Christians, Hindus, Jews, and Muslims, our religious beliefs are still very similar. There have been many religions throughout the past. Most believed in many gods with some evolving into monotheistic religions, but their major beliefs of what gods are have remained much the same. Many have a Zeus like figure who ends up being the supreme being. Most of the time this god or gods are detached from humanity, dwelling in a far off place. These gods have the ability to interact with humanity when necessary but yet keep themselves separate at the same time. They generally demand the respect and adoration of humanity with some frightful curse as a punishment if this adoration isn't given. Most, if not all of them have killed humans for not obeying or for not worshiping them properly. Most have been credited with wiping out humanity in a large way. Many religions have the same stories spun up in a different way to make their god appear more powerful or better in some way than another god. It is kinda the grown up version of the kindergarten playground conversation of "my dad can beat up your dad." Most religions argue that their beliefs are somehow different and better than others and will often claim ultimate authority, and offer redemption of some kind that only their religion can produce. Religions have done this from the dawn of time and continue to do this to this day. Some such as Christianity even contain tens of thousands of denominations inside of it, declaring that others within the very same religion, but yet outside of their denomination, will end up ultimately cursed. Christians can't even agree on what Christianity is. We as a species have not evolved or progressed much in this area, we have mostly just relabeled and regurgitated the same old thing for thousands of years.

If we were to take our societal and religious structures and set them up, side by side next to a timeline beginning around the time of the advent of civilization, they would look very similar. I imagine them to look like the infamous cactus of the American west. Give society, government, and religion its own cactus. They stand tall and strait and only have a couple of arms or branches coming out from the main trunk. The main trunk of the cactus would represent the more ancient or original versions of what we have today. The branches would be representing offshoots and variations from the original societal structure, religion, or formulation. These branches are few and they spring out a short distance from the main trunk, but ultimately turn vertical and grow in the same direction as the main trunk. They look very similar to the main trunk, and essentially gain their life from, and through the main trunk. In fact, if the main trunk or original governmental or religious system were to be brought down or were to die in any way, as flawed or irrelevant in today's world, then all of its offshoots would wither and die along with it. If you try to mess with or alter either of these "cactuses" then you will be met with some very sharp needles. These cactuses have developed these needles as a defense mechanism for just such a reason. They are there for self-preservation. If you attempt to take them down or mess with them in any major way, then you will likely have an immense amount of pain to deal with in the process.

I feel as though some of these systems and societal structures have absolutely crippled us as humans. I feel as though humanity is so lost right now that we are the equivalent of an eagle without wings. It's as if we are descendants of many generations of flightless eagles and we don't even remember that we were ever able to fly. We don't even know that we are supposed to have wings. Could you imagine an eagle that couldn't fly? An eagle is capable of so many great things when it flies. Its very livelihood and wellbeing depend heavily on this characteristic. What could we as humans accomplish if we realized our true potential? Our allegiance to our nationality and religions has cut our wings off and kept us bound to the service of them. We are kept so busy defending these manmade systems that we don't even realize what else we could be doing. It's as if we are down here struggling to survive through all the threats on the ground when we could just fly above it all. I don't necessarily think anyone is intentionally brainwashing anyone. I know this is arguable, however I believe it is more of an ancient tribal survival instinct. It is how our ancestors survived in primeval times and simply has not been reconsidered. This instinct is like an appendage that we no longer need. We as a species may need to re-examine what is necessary and simply let that characteristic of some social and governmental constructs fade away. We could also compare humanity to a group of hikers in a massive national forest that are attempting to navigate a maze of trails. This group has strayed down so many trails that were never intended to be traveled. They have taken so many wrong paths that they don't even know how to backtrack far enough to get onto the correct path. Their maps and everything they thought they knew are completely useless. They need to put their maps down and figure out how to survive long enough to regain their composure and get back on the correct path. The good news is that they are in a group and they can draw from many different experiences and trains of thought. This would be great if the majority of them could realize that they are lost. If they could all agree that they are actually lost, they would need to realize that their different personalities, experiences, forms of processing information and skill sets actually make them stronger. No one person or group of similar people has the one true answer to their problem. This group must realize that the thoughts and ideas of the collective group must be gathered, processed, and correlated. Only then can this group continue moving forward on their journey. If a group of them begins to move and the majority cannot agree that they are even lost then there will be much internal strife and little, if any, progress will be made. Civilizations with power have been so inclined to just force their opinion and way of life on others that I feel as though we have forgotten how to see things from another perspective. To see things from an opposing or different perspective does not automatically mean that you agree. Seeing things from another's perspective only causes you to humanize and respect others. It keeps one from attacking viscously or committing inhumane acts towards others. To have power has simply meant that you could in some way dominate the societies surrounding you and force your viewpoints on others. This always worked well for the nation in power, until another nation became more powerful and forced its viewpoints on them. This has been the same bloody cycle since the dawn of civilization and continues to this day. Nations gaining power, adopting a national religion to unify everyone and enabling them to demonize the "others", and then forcing themselves on those "others".

I believe that at large, the source of mankind's suffering is due to us setting up shop in an environment that we were never meant to exist in. We have become so lost, and we didn't even realize it, and we have chosen to build our home there. Not only did we not realize we were in the wrong environment, but we have erected many social and religious systems and structures from this place of loss. These systems, religions, and various social structures could never fit our true identities because the places they come from are all wrong. Now, because we are living inside systems and structures that are not conducive to realizing our true identity, we begin to live out of frustration because we cannot figure out why joy and happiness are almost unattainable. This in my opinion is where humanity is at this moment. It is a possibility however that mankind formed some of these social constructs because it was the best they could do at the time. They were working with an even more limited source of knowledge than us today. We then took these ancient constructs and cemented them in place, thereby taking away their adaptability. Some of these structures that were cemented in place were very useful for their time, however with their inability to adapt, they became ancient and archaic and serve little usefulness in the modern day. Many religions find themselves in this spot. It was decided upon hundreds or thousands of years ago that the truth as seen at the time, was the ultimate truth, for all time. The stamp of approval was placed on the thoughts, ideas, and writings of the time, and ever since we have been attempting to uphold these ancient ideas. The irony of it all is that these ancient ideas are constantly being bent and modified in an attempt to make them relevant with modern generations. Most of the time the people doing this are shouting that we must return to the religion of old, not realizing that they themselves are bending and twisting ancient meanings to justify their way of thinking. Many of the top religions and governments of our world have become so bent and distorted that they are on the verge of breaking. If some of these religions and governments are to survive then they must become adaptable and the people participating in these systems must approach them in a different way. This is a subject that I intend to dig into deeper later on in this book.

Hopefully this sets the tone and overall expectation for this book. Once again, as a reminder, do not take the things I have said or will say as a dogmatic statement. These are my opinions and viewpoints as I see them now. I normally do not attempt to provide answers to the complexities of society that I see. The intent is to spark an imaginative thought within us all. I am sure that the answers will need to be arrived upon by many brilliant minds, along with much trial and error. Just like the explorers of our world both past and present, their destinations and goals are rarely reached on the first attempt. Sometimes the goal is never reached by the first explorers at all, yet they blazed a trail for others to follow. There were questions in the past of whether it was even possible for humans to reach the highest peaks of earth's mountains. If there were not people such as Mallory, then the answer would undoubtedly be "no". The visions and drive of people such as Mallory literally made it possible for humans to stand on Everest's summit. Now hundreds of people a year reach the summit. Anyone in good health and with enough money can buy a guided excursion to stand on the very peak that many thought was unreachable. The thing of it is, this peak would still be unreachable if everyone were to listen to the critics. Because of Mallory's ambition in the early 1920's a man named Edmund Hillary climbed to the top of Everest in 1953. Another awesome story is the climbing of the north face of the Eiger. Many died attempting it, however Anderl Heckmair was the first successful person to do so back in 1938. It took a whole expedition three days to climb the north wall. In November of 2015 there was a Swiss climber, Ueili Steck who climbed the north face in 2 hours 22 minutes and 50 seconds. Ueli wasn't necessarily a better climber than the climbers of generations past, however the previous generations taught him that climbing the Eiger was possible. He then took his spirit of adventure and the knowledge that a person can climb it, and the routes they used, and focused his attention on being the fastest. His ability to do so was built on the blood sweat and tears of the people who were willing to try something that they were not even sure could be done.

I love the adventurous spirit of our explorers who are willing to risk so much to reach places beyond the limits of our grasp. I think we need to add a new realm to our ideas of exploration. I believe we need to take a more serious look at the exploration of our societal structures and systems and begin to dream of new and great ways of thinking and existing. I think we need to re-explore reality. I, once again, believe that our ability to dream and reach literally unlocks the impossible and makes them possible. I believe we can create possibilities. Anything that is not reached for, will always remain impossible. If it is attempted over and over again, and every possible approach is tried and still the destination remains unattainable then at least we can say we tried. I hope humanity and each individual person never have to reach our end wondering what would have been possible if we had only tried.

May every one of you be blessed for participating in this life and in this existence. In so doing you are in your own way participating in this great endeavor of moving humanity forward to its true potential, even if it is just one foot at a time.

~ Before continuing, I ask that if you have not done so, please go back and read the intro to this book or at least the very last paragraph. I really want people to understand that my intentions are not to belittle or attack any individuals. ~

CHAPTER 2:

GOVERNMENTS
AND NATIONS

OH JEEZ. WHERE DO WE start with this one? Nations and their governments are such a complex subject that I in no way am attempting to explain them or get into too many of them specifically. I am also no expert, and I would simply get in over my head. In a broad sense they have been used to draw "lines in the sand", as it were, to separate one people group from another. From its origins it would have been used to designate one tribal group and their right to resources inside the borders they created. In their day these borders may have created a sense of security and identity. It would have been a way of staking claim to resources to ensure the well-being of that tribe or culture. We have such global capabilities now and technology has advanced in such a way that everyone on the globe could equally benefit from it all without the need to hoard resources for ourselves. Today, the grab for resources around the world is to gain a leverage point in order to usurp power and wealth. We have held on to an ancient tribal survival mechanism that causes us to defend our identity through our nationality rather than through our common humanity. We have taken on the task of propping up government rather than charitably helping our fellow humans. If our identity is always attached to a certain nation or government then we will never be able to see ourselves or others as true humans. Instead, we see ourselves and especially others as entities or products of their governments. We even see other humans as a resource to be obtained, the same way we see things like oil, steel, and diamonds. We tend to gain our identity through external manmade sources rather than finding it within ourselves and other humans. Within our nations and among our own people groups we further find identity in things such as sports and what teams we like the best. We may look to cars and which ones we think are the best or the fastest. I believe lack of identity is a large source, or perhaps THE source for all the evil, depression, anxiety, etc. that we see today. Society and government has handed us things in which to gain a sense of identity, however this only leads to more depravation and anxiety because these things can never reveal who you truly are. Identifying as an American Republican Capitalist or any other national, political, or religious system will never be able to reach the true inner person and identify the nuances within. This will ultimately cause us to look at others outside of our self-made boundaries through a distorted lens. Depression, anxiety, and anger have become so normal in our society, and I believe it comes from a false sense of identity that we have taken on. If we don't know who we truly are, then we also do not have a correct view of our fellow humans. It is not that hard to commit great evils against people that have been diminished in value. We can easily devalue other people if we gain our identity through man made systems of religion and government. This is how nations have so easily demonized others to justify wars and slavery. We have lost our joy because we don't know our true value and we continue to live in an environment that is foreign to our true nature. Cheery and happy people are almost considered abnormal and we kind of look at them funny. I feel like the main contributing factors to this "foreign environment" humans have found ourselves in is made of structures and systems ranging from governments, religion, economic systems all the way down to caste systems, city zoning, what stores we shop in and even the definition of success and the drive for the latest high-tech gadget.

Now all of this is not to say that anyone participating in these systems is a bad person. Actually, it is normally quite the opposite. Most of the time these systems are filled with well-intentioned and loving people who are victims of the very systems they are striving to uphold. For instance, the medieval Catholic friar who taught indulgences as a way to rescue loved ones out of purgatory was normally very innocent to the fact that the indulgence system was manufactured to make the "church" wealthy at the expense of the common people. I know it is very hard to fathom, but the same is true for even a member of the Nazi party in the World War II. There were many common Nazi soldiers who honestly believed they were on the right side of history and had good intentions to rid the world of evil. Some had no idea how evil the system was that they were serving. Some did not know about the pure evil hatred that drove some of the founders of these systems. The crazy part is that pure hatred towards another can easily be disguised as love. Love for your country, family, religion, or the very last stitch of a free society left in the world. It is portrayed as a system and cause that is worthy of devotion greater than valuing and loving our fellow human beings, and even greater than ourselves. This is all true for many if not all the atrocities committed throughout history. Governmental systems and structures such as Rome, Syria, various warlords, Christians, Muslims, the Crusades, the Nazis, ISIS, the USA, China, Russia, Communism and yes even Democracy have demanded such unquestionable devotion that it has clouded the eyes of its servants. You end up serving this idea or entity with such fervent devotion that you overlook the needs of humanity in order to continually prop up this fabricated system. Most of the time these fabricated systems have been erected with only a certain nation or people group in mind. If constructed this way, it often requires the sacrifice and suffering of the people left on the outside. It often requires you to take away the rights and freedoms of another in order to preserve your own. It still requires the ancient ritual of human blood sacrifice.

I don't believe that the world and our lives are just one big conspiracy theory with everything being contrived from an evil heart. Although some of that may be true, I believe that some of the flawed and destructive systems were contrived by well-intentioned people, and it was simply taken to a level it either never should have gone to or was never intended go to in the first place. Let's use the conquest and foundation of the USA as an example. The move to the "New World" was in general something that was done in innocence by many of the people. Many came to escape a life of persecution, enslavement, and poverty. Many were just sick and tired of their current existence and were willing to try anything for a fresh start. This is not necessarily a bad thing or a bad place to be in. What ended up happening though was that the thirst and hunger for freedom and adventure was held to such high esteem that it led to the extermination of many of the local indigenous people of the Americas. The need and drive for freedom and adventure is not a bad thing, but when it comes at the expense of another then it requires a step back and thorough reexamination. The people who did this were wanting very innocent things for their loved ones and people within their groups, however they were so focused on their dreams and visions they were willing to snuff out the lives of others to get it. The people coming to America were also products of the systems they served back in Europe. These systems essentially made it ok to have a cause greater in value than other human beings. Many came as a group and found their identity in this group. They had such identity entangled in other things that it caused them to overlooking the humanity of the ones they killed. The system they came from taught them that anyone that was not like them was of inferior existence and could be exploited to increase the dominance of their own people. They sought survival through the extermination of others. They were taught that you escaped persecution by attaining power. By attaining power, you would then persecute the ones you had power over. The governmental and religious history of Europe prior to the settlement of the Americas proves this to be true. This mentality reigned true throughout the "civilized" world. Unfortunately, this idea and method of attaining is still prevalent in our society to this day. After the foundation of the United States, many set out to create a nation of prosperity and freedom. Once again this was not a bad thing, however the methods used were grotesque. Many attained their freedoms and blessings through the enslavement of others. How ironic is that? A nation was so focused on their own freedom and prosperity that it was willing to enslave and impoverish others in order to get it. This methodology can still be seen today even in our ideas of freedom of speech and religion. We often say that we want freedom of speech, but what we really mean is that we want freedom to voice OUR opinions yet we demonize others for voicing theirs. We want to be able to voice our opinions but ridicule anyone with a different opinion. You don't need to look any further than our "left vs right" politics. We say we want freedom of religion. We say we want to bring prayer back in school, but if we hear a Muslim prayer in a school, we lose our minds. If we see a Muslim or Hindu practicing their religion in public then we get all defensive and wonder what this country is coming to. What our country really means when we say that we want freedom of speech and religion is that we want freedom to say what WE want and freedom to practice OUR religion. Honestly though, we don't care about your rights or freedoms, we just want ours. When the same practice of silencing voices and religions is used against us and our religion then we cry "persecution!" People say they want religion back in government, but when a Muslim reaches office, they want that person ejected from office and talk about how America is going down hill. We want our prayer and OUR religion back in office. We don't care about yours. Actually, we think your prayer and religion is evil and should be kept silent. This of course is said in jest and is only for proving a point.

Once again, I am not saying that humanity's governmental systems started out as inherently evil. Some of these things such as government may have actually started out rather nicely and out of necessity. I am also not saying that absolutely no government is necessary. We just may need to re-think how to implement it. At the dawn of humanity there may have been some very basic guidelines set in place for the "betterment of the herd". Systems very primal and animalistic. It may have been guidelines that were implemented because some were better hunters and others better gatherers. It may have started out to ensure that everyone pulls their own fair share of the load. When it comes to a means of survival, you can't have too many people not producing. If hunters were to bring their freshly killed game of the day and the gatherers were to bring their plant material into the camp and it is all to be shared for the common good of everyone, then you can't have too many people who consistently do nothing (and please do not apply today's politics to this). Eventually this could have led to punishment for stepping outside of your assigned place, or for one not carrying their load. Once this happened enough, there was suddenly a "need" to have a system to deal with people not staying in line. You now need manpower to enforce rules and guidelines. If you need manpower to enforce, then you need manpower to oversee as well. Throw in a couple leaders with ill intent and the desire for power, and suddenly you have governments arise. Certain people groups in various times and places around the globe developed certain beliefs in different deities. Individual societies begin to bloom from there. As these progress and the snowball gets bigger and bigger we end up with feudal systems, lords, kings, Democracies, Republics and Communism. We end up with a hodgepodge of governments and religions. As a side note; I know my examples are very oversimpli-fied and do not cover nearly all the details, and they are not intended to. They are merely intended to paint a general picture in one's head. I am sure there are specialists in social studies and anthropology that would have quite a bit of input here, but let's not get caught in the weeds. Now all of these things such as social boundaries and beliefs may not be altogether bad when there are small nomadic groups wondering the planet. The problems arise when these small groups begin to grow and bump into each other. If you respect the other group and their uniqueness, then all is well. The issues arise if even one group believes that its way of being is the only way to be. If on group believes other groups should be as they are, then you begin to have problems. When one group thinks they have the right to the resources within the border of another group. When hoarding of resources becomes prevalent in a group. Then you will begin to see instances of a people group imposing its power and values onto another people group. Once this happens you must instantly have systems of government and control. Now suddenly you can go from a very peaceful and carefree lifestyle, to a civilization full of rigid rules, laws, and religion. They begin to gain their identity through their group and the things they have developed. You will have the rise of militant societies. I personally believe that the dawn of government and religion both spring from the need to control others. This is the conundrum that we find ourselves in today, except it is now on steroids and bigger than ever. The world has come to a place where the most intolerant governmental and religious systems have beaten and strong armed the other more tolerant ones out. On top of that, you now have these intolerant systems grinding up against each other due to rising populations, increased travel, and various other technological advancements. We have very intolerant systems that are being forced into very close proximity with each other and even forced to deal with and accept these other systems, and it is not going so well. Now in the past and up to the present, a very normal thing to do was to just keep beating these "others" out, even if it meant eradication through violence. This however, due to humanity's continued evolvement, is becoming less and less acceptable. It is still practiced to a degree if it can be masked behind a more acceptable movement. Now humanity is coming into a place where acceptance of others is our only other option. Governments will do as government does, but people in general are becoming less accepting of just lording it over other people.

So where do we go from here? Do we need to do a major re-structuring of our current systems? Do we need to totally eradicate some systems all together? Are all systems bad or are some systems a necessity to preserve human existence? I don't know the answer to these questions. I don't want to give yet another guide to structuring another system to add to the droves of systems we already have. I just want to provoke thought and spark the imagination. After all, small ideas and "light bulb moments" are the birth places of things that change the world. I also do not believe that one person, society, continent, can come up with the right answer. It will be a collective thought shared and communicated the world over. Many of the world's most prominent governments and societies will need to learn to speak less and give other societies room to speak and express their viewpoints.

I believe that the ideas and experiences of everyone need to be taken into account in order to move humanity forward. What my intent is, is to point out that many religions and nationalistic nations across the globe have ceased from taking advice or ideas from anything that is not inside of their circle. I believe that our major governments and religions that dominate the world are largely here because they were the more aggressive ones of their time and simply strong armed their way into power. Less aggressive or less militant systems would have just become absorbed or forcefully eradicated. Going back to the European conquest of the Americas and the eradication of many native tribes, religions, and traditions. There were many tribes and their cultures who were quite literally wiped off the planet with their rich cultures forever lost in time.

My context in life has been drawn from an American Christian viewpoint. We as Americans and Christians have largely engrained the idea within our nation and religion the notion of being exceptional. We believe that we stand head and shoulders above anyone that is not inside either one of those two circles. This in my opinion is next to indisputable. Look at our politics and our willingness to place "America first" at the expense of other nations. I recently had a couple of major wakeup calls concerning my nationalism that ended in a huge disillusionment. Nationalistic beliefs were almost harder to dismantle within myself than those of my religion, however both were so closely intertwined that for me to reconsider one, I had to reconsider the other. One thing tied into nationalism for me was the idea of "American Exceptionalism". Oftentimes, when one goes through a spiritual type of reworking, there is a major domino effect. There was no exception in my case. Reconsidering not only my religious beliefs but also my moral beliefs inevitably led to questioning many different things since my previous religious beliefs had caused me to be rather callous towards other people. It was especially true of my view of other nations and religions that my government and religion had told me were bad or dangerous. Due to my shedding of a religion that by default told me I was exceptional solely because I was a part of that religion, inevitably caused me to question whether I was exceptional strictly because of the nation I was born in to. Since I no longer believed I was anything special solely based on what I believed, I was able to look at humanity and other nations, religions and people groups as being equal to myself. I was able to see them with the same respect I had for my fellow Americans. I could begin to love people. I know this sounds like I was a very messed up individual and that I believed some very messed up things. That is because I WAS messed up and I DID believe some very nasty things. That is exactly my point. I considered myself a very good person, and I was. I simply could not see through the vail of religion and nationalism that was draped over my eyes. I did want what was best for everyone. I was just misguided in thinking that what we American Christians had was what everyone else needed. My experience is that in a large way, this had been engrained in my belief system because the Christianity and Americanism I was involved in both taught me that I was exceptional and ultimately superior because I was a part of both systems. The scary part was that I didn't even know that I looked down on other nationalities and religions. You see, American Nationalism (any nationalism for that matter) taught me that because I was born inside these lines drawn on a map, I have a superiority to those that are not living inside of those same lines. We can know this to be true by simply seeing how we treat others outside of these borders, not to mention how we have treated "others" inside of our borders. We say that the rights we hold as true for Americans are basic human rights that all humans should enjoy. We don't truly believe this because we do not grant those same rights to people living only a couple of feet outside of our borders. Suddenly when you are on the outside of these borders, you don't deserve the same treatment as I do. We even practice this in our foreign affairs very blatantly by leading with an "America First" doctrine. This was another major wake up for me when our leader, the very one that was the champion of my very own political party ran on this moto. This "make America great again" by placing "America First" propaganda essentially meant that we as America could do anything we wanted to another nation as long as it was for our benefit, and we went nuts with glee at the thought of it. By this time, my views were changing, and the reality of this seemed to smack me in the face. It was shocking. We could exploit the Middle East if it meant that my gas would cost me a dollar less per gallon than the week before. Our nation has quite literally invaded another country, killing tens of thousands, mostly for power and resources. We could exploit Africa for diamonds and cobalt if it meant I could live in luxury.

American Christianity teaches us almost the same things as well. I am exceptional and "saved" because I am within the Christian borders. All those on the outside will ultimately be damned. This is why Christianity has worked so well for many nations. It can easily be used to prop up government, and just as easily be used to demonize and wage war on others. Now the same as Americanism, Christianity says that we all deserve the same things and that we are all "children of God", yet we ultimately believe that those on the outside are not as exceptional as me. They will, after all, ultimately be damned at some point and time. As a matter of fact, I would say that Americanism and American Christianity are so similar that the one cannot exist without the other. If America would ever reach its end, then so would Western Christianity. Many even call it American Christianity. America as a domineering nation could not exist without American Christianity. You simply could not teach this type of exceptionalism and nationalism without our version of Christianity. As a matter of fact, the American continents could not have even been exploited and settled in the way that they were with-out Christianity as its driving force. You simply could not justify and rally enough public support to invade, steal lands, enslave and con-duct mass genocide on another people group without such an influ-ential religion as Christianity. It was a textbook "copy and paste" from the Israelite conquest of Canaan. This place was portrayed as the promised land and the inhabitants must be evangelized. If the natives did not convert, then they were considered subhuman and could be dispatched almost at will. This was almost identical to the Israelite context of killing all who were not like them due to the claim that they would be a "thorn in Israel's side" if they were not eliminated. Many biblical passages blame Israel's troubled time from the disobedient action of not killing everyone they conquered. The injustice to the indigenous tribes of America continues to this day. Boarding Schools that remained open into the modern times, well within the memory of not so old people, were responsible for the mistreatment and death of countless indigenous people. Furthermore, I had thought that America only stood for what was right for all of humanity. I had no idea how wrong I was. I began looking into the racial injustices of America, and I was thoroughly shocked and appalled. I had obviously known about slavery in America and of course knew that slavery was wrong. I considered it a major black eye in American history, however I had no clue how bad it really was. The injustices went way beyond the Civil War. There are people still alive today that could remember the public lynching's of African Americans in this country. I could finally see the corralling and controlling of African Americans through "Red Lining", the war on drugs and the American prison system. I found out how African Americans were used to keep American companies going during our wars, just to be driven out and left jobless after the white soldiers came home and were in need of employment. Have you ever asked yourself how African Americans were used in Southern rural plantations, but ended up scattered throughout the inner cities all across America? If you do not know the answer, then consider looking into it. This book is not intent on going into all the fine details. You could write books about this stuff, and I am no expert. I am just in the process of uncovering it for myself. As an American you owe it to yourself and others to know the true history that is not taught in schools. Indeed it is a nasty history and you can easily see why our nation did not want this stuff to be public knowledge. A nation cannot create a good nationalistic people if such ugly truths are taught to its citizens. It is very hard to admit as a patriotic person that America was not really built, and in the place that it is now, on hard work and an unquenchable desire to succeed. It is here rather largely on the exploitation, enslavement and murder of other people groups. Most of our "blessings" were carried in on the backs of those we enslaved. Don't get me wrong, we did and still do have many honest, hard working citizens. My neighbors and fellow citizens truly are good people. Many are simply unaware of our true past. My point is that we would never have so quickly reached a place of global dominance if we had cohabitated with the natives and if we had not enslaved other people. Much of our early history is completely unjustifiable, and yet somehow it was justified through nationalism and religion.

I had another very eye-opening moment when I was reading an article on the Soviet Union's invasion of Czechoslovakia back in the late 60's. In this article it showed Soviet soldiers riding on an armored vehicle with a crowd of angry Czechs screaming and spitting at them. The look on the Soviet soldier's faces were that of disbelief and bewilderment. What I did not know was that the Soviet Union looked at itself as "freedom dealers" the same way America did. Much of this is brought about through their version of Eastern Orthodox Christianity. They thought they were bringing freedom and prosperity to the Czech nation. The Soviet soldiers thought these citizens would be happy to see them and would celebrate their victory. These Soviet soldiers could not figure out why in the world these Czechs were so angry at them. This absolutely blew me away that Soviet soldiers would also think of themselves as "the good guys" attempting to rid the world of injustice and bringing freedom to others. It blew my mind. It was always taught to me that they were the bad guys attempting to take away freedom. It was so engrained in me that I never had the thought that they would considered themselves good. I mean it quite literally when I say that it never entered my brain. It is amazing how two nations as similar as the Soviet Union and the United States could so strongly appose each other when we both thought we were doing the same things. Our governments simply taught each's respective citizens that they were on the right side of the issue. Both even used Christianity to bolster their nationalism. American soldiers looked at ourselves the same way when we went into Iraq as these Soviet soldiers did in Czechoslovakia. Sure some Iraqis were happy to have us there, but most were not. A lot of Iraqis were happy to see Saddam Hussein leave power, but they didn't want us to stay there. I couldn't figure this out and it was very disheartening to see the anger and hatred directed at us. Afterall, we were bringing freedom, liberty, and democracy to an oppressed people. Now Saddam Hussein undoubtedly did some very nasty things to people and probably justified this through a religion such as Islam, but ultimately, I grew to see our invasion of Iraq as another American conquest. Think about it. If we had a horrendous government in America and another nation came into the United States and toppled our government. We would at best tip our hats and say "thank you, now go home". That would be best case scenario, especially if, on top of everything, it were an Islamic nation that did it. What would we do if they just tried settling in here and attempted to establish a government different from anything we ever knew before? It wouldn't go over well. We preached a better life for the Iraqi people, but that's not what it was about. Why else would we try so hard to force our own type of government on another nation when many people didn't want us there? If we do this on a personal level, then is this not called assault? If it was about helping the people of Iraq, would we not just topple their corrupt government and then simply be available to help facilitate what they truly wanted? After all they just want a good safe life for themselves and their loved ones the same as we do. This lifestyle they want may not look exactly the same as it does here, but they want the same end result. We live halfway around the world and on a completely different continent, separated by oceans, with a completely different culture. Now if you can reason this out to say they couldn't do this to us, but we can or are allowed do it to them as if we have some special right, then isn't that exceptionalism? Is this not viewing ourselves with a sense of superiority? If you say "absolutely and we deserve that superiority", for any number of reasons, then how can you believe in our very core values of "all men being created equal"? Do we only mean Americans and only men or do we truly mean all people? Do we really believe in the equality of all people or does it just sound good and make us feel better? In order for a nation to be different, it cannot simply have nice words in its pledge or national anthem. This nation needs the action behind the words, otherwise these words are empty and serve to only make us feel exceptional. I do not believe that America has truly exemplified this as of yet. We in America preach diversity and yet we want everyone to look and act like us. We do not truly see the strength of a diverse humanity. We say that we do, but honestly, I do not believe that we do.

Another eye-opening moment was when I was watching a documentary about the meltdown of Chernobyl, a Soviet nuclear power plant, that occurred in 1986. This was such a major disaster that they had to evacuate nearby towns and cities. The propaganda blaring through the loudspeakers was that of encouragement to not stop fighting for freedom and justice. They once again thought of themselves the way that Americans did, as the bringers of freedom and justice. I am sure that in their minds, we Americans were portrayed as the evil ones who were out to steal away all that was good and right. I mean why not? You cannot unify a people group behind a government without giving them an evil enemy and telling them that they are in a fight to defend all things good. The glue that always holds it together is religion. For the Soviets this was largely the Eastern Orthodox strain of Christianity.

So what are we doing to each other? Why is it so hard to see that we humans all essentially the same? We all generally just want to have a nice life, free of oppression with the ability to explore and thrive as we desire. Another person or people group's creativity should not be seen as a threat, but as another thread in the tapestry that binds us together. All the threads in a tapestry are not always the same. The most beautiful ones are comprised of many different colors all woven together to make beautiful designs. In fact, once a tapestry is created, one would ruin it if you tried to separate all the different threads. Is it possible for us to place nations and politics to the side and live together in a way that is truly becoming of us all? Can we stop gaining our identities through our nations and religion? Can we stop looking at each other across borders and oceans and see a common humanity in everyone? It is funny how we have attempted to subjugate others and attempt to force assimilate races into our own in order to make "them" like "us" and we are still comprised of thousands of ethnicities. It is impossible to gain sameness through force. We have tried to make everyone like "us" or eliminate those who refuse, and yet we are as diverse as ever. Don't you think there is a different and better way to live together?

CHAPTER 3:

NATIONALISM
VS. PATRIOTISM

I CAN IMAGINE THAT THERE are many Americans saying that I hate America and would also say that I am not patriotic. Personally, I believe many people are nationalistic and hide it under the cloak of patriotism. I believe that there is a very big difference between nationalism and patriotism. Many Americans ride around with the American flag on their truck and a sticker on their back window that says "Patriot" but could more easily be translated "Nationalist". I believe many Americans have become nationalistic and call it patriotism. In my view, Nationalism would be claiming an allegiance to a certain governmental entity, even to the detriment and exclusion of other nations and people groups. Nationalism would place its nation first above other nations. Nationalism leads with "America First" slogans. Nationalism would support the exploitation of another nation to improve its own gas prices. Nationalism would cause you to fight your fellow neighbor in order to uphold the system of government you believe is the correct one. Patriotism on the other hand is about people and seeking their best interests, but not at the expense of another. If government is present, it should never seek its own best interest. Nationalism enters the picture if government requires allegiance to it over fellow humans. Patriotism should not exclude anyone regardless of who they are or where they come from. Patriotism would be more about trying to make the lives of your fellow citizens better from within and not at the expense of another nation. You do what you can from within with what you have available to you. My blessings should never be carried in on the backs of other people. In a simple way, and on a micro level I would use my current town of residence as an example. I live in small town USA, and I absolutely love where I live. The town is quiet, safe, and the people here are almost always friendly. The community is tight and the town has many functions for its residents. I really feel as though my family and I belong here. I love the town I live in because of the people that are in it and the community they created. I do not live in this town because of the town government or officials. I actually know very little about the town officials. Now the government can help facilitate the goals that the citizens are trying to reach. They can work with the visions of its people to help create the environment that they want in their community. What I have seen is that the town's people will do a lot to help improve the lives of their neighbors. Now generally one town cannot exploit a neighboring town so that the livelihood of its own residents can be improved. We all know this would be wrong. We can see this because the next town over is just as American as the town I live in. Once again, I love my town because of the people that are in it, not because of its government. It is true that a government may be able to help facilitate an environment, but it cannot create it. I would absolutely support the town government if it truly serves, cares for and supports its citizens or the citizens of a neighboring town. I would stop supporting my town government if it stiff-armed neighboring communities to make my life better. If another family must suffer for my well-being, then I would no longer support that. I want what is best for the people around me and humanity in general. If the town officials would start being not so nice to another town, I would suddenly be very concerned about what it is doing. If it continued, I would actually oppose this towns government, but I would continue supporting the people around me as much as I could. If the government of my town becomes tyrannical, am I patriotic in my support of that government or am I patriotic when I support the people suffering under the government? Supporting a tyrannical government does not make you patriotic. Is this in fact not patriotism in its true form, when you care for those around you? If patriotism is in fact support of the government regardless of its actions, then people need to know when to stop being patriotic. Can we expand this to a greater national level? If we can see that I cannot exploit a neighboring town because they are fellow citizens of the United States, then why can we not see that another nation's citizens are just as much citizens of this earth as I am? If so, then if a town cannot exploit, invade, or enslave a neighboring town, then why can we do this to another nation or people group? We are a global community the same way that we are a local community. Should we then not also do the same in supporting our fellow citizens by speak up against the injustices of our national governments? To want and seek what is best for humanity as a whole is patriotism.

I believe that in order to truly see the humanity in all people around the globe, and in order to consider everyone equal then one must shed any form of religion and nationalism that preaches exceptionalism through the exclusion of others. In fact, I would say that you cannot take advantage of another person or nation unless you somehow justify an exceptional view of yourself. Most of the time national and religious borders are used to do this. Nationalistic people oppress other nations, patriotism doesn't. In my opinion, nationalism needs to be eliminated from our DNA. Patriotism may still have a place, though some would debate this as well. If in fact a person defines nationalism and patriotism as the same thing then we just need to get rid of both. You must look at another human as a lesser being in order to enslave or exploit that person. It is time that humanity begins to look at each other without filters. We cannot continue to look at each other through borders of any kind if we wish to see each other as equals. We cannot continue to see each other in terms of nationality, gender, or religion if we are to progress. This does not mean we cannot respect and acknowledge people for who they are, we just cannot make judgements based on manmade systems. Does this mean that no borders are necessary? I am once again not the one to come up with an answer for this, however if you gain any sense of superior identity because of the borders you find yourself within, then you must re-imagine what a border is for and how it is to be used?

CHAPTER 4:

HOW DO WE DO THIS?

MANY PEOPLE WHO THINK OF change in major social systems and governmental structures normally envision change being made through massive legislation. Most of the time it is envisioned as dualistic in a sort of good vs. evil type of showdown. Normally this comes with one side kind of forcing their legislation onto another group that doesn't really like it. I do not really believe most legislation is really concerned with the wellbeing of other, but is more of a power grab. I believe this type of change is still more of a power struggle, with one side attempting to gain more power in government in order to force their world view onto someone else. I believe there is a much more fruitful and gentler way for things to change. Change may need to be something that comes more through the changing of society over time. Something to where society simply begins doing things differently, simply because it has progressed in that direction. Some of this may happen fairly quickly, such as over a couple of years, because society has been progressing, yet our dualistic way of doing things has held us back. When the power struggle diminishes, some change could happen quickly because of the stored up energy waiting to be released. When we get beyond dualism, we could see some change catch up to where society already is on the inside. I believe sudden change through political violence of action has actually stagnated our society. When world views and religious beliefs are perceived to be under attack by massive and sudden legislative change, many people understandably push back with the same or greater force. Sometimes this leads to deadlock. Both sides of an argument wanting change, yet becoming unyielding with the fear of giving an inch and somehow losing a mile. This causes society to become stuck in a rut for many years. Sudden change such as if legislated could tear the rug out from under people. Sudden legislative change could break people. This is all about people. If we take our focus off of people, it all becomes about systems and structures that care very little about anyone. These systems and structures have no morality. These systems and structures vilify people across the aisle, and serve to desensitize us. It causes us to see each other as something less than what we truly are. We should not look to destroy people, but rather to do things in a more gentle way with the intent of preserving as many as possible. We could all believe that what we all really want at our core, as human beings, is not that different. If we could realize that many of the things that are such pillars in our beliefs have been placed there by systems struggling for power, we may be able to look past them more easily.

The fight between left vs. right and good vs. evil has been a fabrication of both religion and government. Normally these two were working together hand in hand and for the same things. Religion and government are essentially two empires occupying the same space that have simply figured out how to use each other to get what they want. By keeping a population fighting over things they will never win is exactly what gives both entities a position in our world. By believing that one or the other is truly pushing to right some kind of wrong that a person truly believes in is exactly what our major systems rely on. In America, our two party system totally relies on major issues in order to survive. Issues such as the second amendment and abortion have become such polarizing subjects. Conservative government and religion need the abortion issue to remain alive and well in order to have something to campaign against. The more liberal government and religion need the second amendment to stay alive and well for the same reason. Both parties created these issues. Both parties NEED these issues to keep constituents wound up, fighting to gain power. They actually need the issues they claim to be fighting, to stay alive and well. If either party actually fixed the problem, they would lose major leverage points. Furthermore, if they keep each party's constituents focused on their one big thing, they keep the focus off of many other things that could be way more important. The thing of it is that both parties have no intention of bringing true change in either subject, nor can they. Division and unrest are exactly what keeps any powerful entity in its place of power. Both religion and government thrive on a divided and disturbed populace. Government is very good at suppressing violence. If a government can maintain a small level of violence among the populace, it will always have a job to do, and will look like it is more of a necessity than what it really is. Government will quite literally create problems to give us something to fight against if a problem is not naturally present already. If we conservatives believe our liberties are hinged on having our guns, if we choose to make this the hill we die on, then all other liberties can be eroded without much attention from us. If we liberals claim the same about abortion rights, then the same will happen there as well. With the populace divided, and each with their focal points, the government is seen as a necessity in a struggle of good vs evil. If society would simply care about the wellbeing of the people around them in a "here and now" mentality, and forget their political talk points, almost all political issues would dissolve. If people were present and truly cared to see each other thrive (not through legislation) then the issues of violence and death would essentially disappear. As long as we look at each other through political and religious lenses then we will always be stuck in a cycle of hatred and death.

We must remove the idea of human sacrifice from our society. We think people must be sacrificed in order to achieve whatever agenda we wish to accomplish. Human sacrifice has been a thing that ranges back to the dawn of civilization. Today we normally do not take one to a literal alter and sacrifice them. Today human sacrifice has taken on many different forms, and is still alive and well. When a person is beheaded in the name of Islam, when an American soldier dies on the altar of freedom, when the idea of prosperity comes through the exploitation of another, this is all human sacrifice. When we believe that another must have less so that I can have more, this is human sacrifice. People wasting their lives away at jobs they hate in order to keep a system or enterprise going is human sacrifice. The idea that a human life must be squandered away to keep anything afloat or to prosper another is sacrificing that human's life on the altar of a fabricated society.

You should never force someone out of their comfort zone so that you can remain in yours. Your blessings arriving on the backs of another human is in fact not a blessing, but rather slavery and subjugation. My cheap gas prices should never come because we oppressed another society. I should not complain about high gas prices in America, when the cost is twice as high in another nation. Why complain about gas prices and inflation if I have the blessing of not having a T-72 tank sitting in my street? We have been perpetuating these forms of sacrifice throughout history with no signs of stopping. Anytime you find these ideas you either have religion, nationalism, greed, or narcissism as the driving force. I am not talking about someone giving up something from themselves willingly to help another. That is charity. I am talking about elements of society that takes advantage of another human in the form of forced necessity. In Native American cultures you really do not see any of this when they lived as communal tribes. Only when they established permanent "civilized" sites did you find human sacrifice. Yes even Native America has a dark underbelly. Only in established cities such as Cahokia on the Mississippi River and those in among the Aztec cities do you find things such as human sacrifice. This was determined to come from the rise of the need to have a ruling figure or an elite society among commoners. These rulers were often portrayed as having special powers or even as godlike figures. Religions with gods were needed to control the common people, and of course, a person with special access to these gods were also needed. If a powerful person or group takes charge of any population, they need answers and some sort of control for all the things that happen around them. Afterall, if you hold no special benefit or power for the people, then why would they ever need you? If you are to be perceived as a person of authority, you needed a special quality not found in anyone else. Special access to the divine world was often the ticket. If a bountiful harvest was brought in that year, it needed to be because you pleased a god. If there was a drought or flood that led to famine, then it was because you displeased a god, and the population needed to set that right. A person claiming special access to this god or gods was then necessary. Often times a penalty or payment for the negative actions was required to set things right again. If humans created the problem, then often payment through sacrifice was the supposed corrective or pleasing action that was required. The highest payment was a human sacrifice. Plant and animal sacrifice could keep the gods appeased and atone for small offenses, but when real payment was required, it was found in the blood of humans. This is an archaic practice, and most of today's religions are fundamentally founded upon it. For most religions (all the Abrahamic ones), if you took away human sacrifice, the religions would lose all of their meaning. They quite literally would not exist without human blood sacrifice.

For the most part, the degradation of other humans comes about under current societal, governmental, and class structures. Only through the need to have power and possessions, through a poverty mentality do we get such horrible things as we have seen throughout history.

People have been motivated by money, material possessions, power, and fear for most of known history. These things have been used to maintain power, keep economies going, and "make a living" for so long that I think we have a hard time imagining an existence where that would not be necessary. We quite literally cannot imagine an existence without it. One question might be, "who would come repair my roof or fix my car if we didn't have people at regular jobs?" I of course do not have specific details to how it would all work, but I do have examples of how some of it may look. One thing that the Amish community exemplifies very well is community. If someone in their community is in need of anything, whether it is medical care or a new barn, they will make sure they receive it. I have been blessed to have an Amish background. It is also my wife's family background. I have witnessed and participated in building sheds, pouring concrete, replacing roofing, and remodeling homes just through family or community workdays. Community members are quick to give aid if someone falls ill or has a debilitating accident, sometimes stepping in and making sure the family can have all their daily duties taken care of without a hiccup. These were not dreaded or overly laborious tasks. People were happy to help, and people came with smiles and food and had a grand time socializing and working together. There were often so many people that the workload on each individual was quite light. No one required a salary or payment of any kind, and people were united in a common goal. It often served to bring family and community closer together. My point to this is, how energetically would a community come together to help each other out, on whatever task they had, if society and economy were not draining their energy at jobs and such? There are highly energetic people who always want something to do. In fact, if you gave your average couch potato a vision and purpose worth participating in, this person would probably become more energetic than ever imagined before. Do you know how many people love farming or just growing gardens, but they either can't afford it or don't have the time for it? There would be more food than you could shake a stick at if people could truly pursue their passions. "What about my television and smart phone?" some may ask. I don't know. I do not have the answers for some things. Maybe there would be a way to produce those too. Maybe we wouldn't need to have our brains numbed by them at the end of the day if we were happily living a meaningful life. I bet most people's televisions would rot in a corner if they were able to be out intermingling with a true sense of happiness and accomplishments. I'm not knocking tech gadgets by any means, I just think many people use them as a tool to unwind in a way that would not be necessary in a more care free society. If society wasn't structured so horribly, we would not need to escape from it. Maybe there are somethings we would choose to eliminate because their benefit does not outweigh the turmoil that is needed to have it. Do we really need cars with display screens bigger than some TVs in the past? Do we need campers to escape our lives if we have lives that we love living? If we go camping, do we really need to pull a whole house on wheels to the campsite? I know our kids get grumpy and agitated if they have too much "screen time". They often complain if the TV needs to be turned off, but they become much happier shortly thereafter if we go on a walk together. If someone does thrive on a certain business, then could they have that business, and have it be run in a more charitable way rather than draining the energy of its workers to benefit only the top echelon of the company? If you think of it, it is almost another version of slavery. I do not mean that business owners are slave owners. I just mean that our economies can in a way keep people enslaved to it. What if people had the time and energy to pour into community? If people were not so taxed by their jobs and other constructs then how much more willing would people be to pour themselves into the people around them? I even remember back in my evangelical days that I desired to help people out, but my job took my extra energy and the church wanted not only 10% of my entire paycheck, but also wanted 10% of my time. Suddenly I couldn't even help anyone out in need because all of my resources were depleted elsewhere. I think that once people got ahold of a true sense of community, if they had an opportunity to display skill and generosity through general love of others, we could probably get more accomplished more efficiently than before. If a community wants you present simply because they want you as a person, you would be happy to help any way you could. Everyone needs a sense of accomplishment. Would that sense of accomplishment be motivation enough? We have used money and possessions as motivators to get people to produce or do something. We often think that if this were not the case we couldn't accomplish anything as a society. I disagree. I think this method of motivation is actually one of the least efficient motivators. Everyone needs a purpose, and I think so many people struggle to find that purpose in todays failed systems. Having a job to go stamp out brake parts for a car, or to go into the food industry where people are way overworked, and way underpaid just simply isn't worth it. The only way this serves as motivation is because people feal as though it is necessary for survival. Today we do not face a labor shortage. We have plenty of skilled people who are happy to provide for people. Our problem, rather, is that we have a charity and morality shortage. We have a shortage of compensation, a shortage of worker appreciation, a shortage of sense of purpose, and we have an excess of greed and narcissism in corporations and various entities. People are simply not willing to go waste their life away at pointless jobs anymore. If you want the help of today's society you have to appreciate them and give them a true sense of purpose. I say good for them! They are totally right and completely justified in their demand of it too.

I think as society moves forward, our borders, from small to large will shift from things used to separate, to things that can bring the world together. Borders do not need to go away when they are used to highlight cultures. I think there is a difference when a nation creates borders to separate themselves from the world, in order to hoard resources and claim exceptionalism, to having more natural "borders" that help distinguish cultures. For instance, I do not want borders to come down so that global cultures will be exactly the same. I believe that cultural heritages should not be eliminated to bring yet more forced conformity to the world's population. The uniqueness of cultures should be preserved in order to share that uniqueness with the universe. Diversity is something to be cherished, not something to be eliminated. As such, there may need to be some sense of boundaries for these cultural groups, not as a wall to keep people out, but rather as a place one can step in to consciously to celebrate another culture. If I wish to celebrate with aboriginal peoples in my continent and around the world, I need to have a way of finding them, and a way of knowing when I have arrived. A "border" of sorts can give me an awareness, can provide me with a conscious decision to enter into and participate with another culture. These borders may not even be lines on a map. I do not know what they would look like, but all I know is that I do not want everyone across the planet to look and act the same. I just want us to have the freedom to live together without pain or competition. We do not need to remove cultural differences we just need to stop taking advantage of cultures for personal, political, and national gain. We need to stop using borders as points of separation, and use them as places to highlight. We need to be proud of ethnic diversity and share it with the world. We must go out and intermingle with diversity so that we can admire it and see the beauty in it. Forced integration, conformity, and anti-diversity only serves nations and selfish power. This is exactly what we see with colonialism. We should all be aware of the damage that colonialism has caused around the world.

Furthermore, our kids and most adults have never had the time, quietness, and brain space required to figure out who we truly are or what they really want to do. We have been moved from school to work without true contemplation. There has been such a sense of urgency to "produce" that we have overlooked our need to be human. We have been transformed into more of a machine, another resource used to feed hungry systems around the world. As I made my way through life, I had ideas of where I wanted to take my career and my life. The only thing that I found when I got there though was that I still was not happy. I achieved goals, but yet found out time and again that those goals were not true to me as a person. I have worked on farms, been in the military, built homes, owned my own business, moved into sales, and when things set-tled down at each location I realized that nothing really changed inside me. I was still a miserable person. I had been pursuing what society told me I should be pursuing. There was such a pressure to work and be productive that I started working when I was still in school. A job was readily handed to me before I ever had the time to get to know who I truly was. I entered into marriage before I had the chance to know myself. Most people never have the solitude and quietness that is required to truly know themselves and their inner desires. We have been too busy producing and working for something other than ourselves, to even question if the world's systems are even necessary, or configured as they should be. We just methodically and unquestioningly move through life like machines with no real happiness or sense of true purpose. We are more or less taught when to get an education, when to settle down, when to work, when to marry. Most of the time this sequence happens very rapidly, with little to no break in between. We are supposed to choose a carrier, and find a partner to share our lives with, all without the true time and contemplation required to really figure this out. Once caught up inside the system, all available brain space is used in maintaining a job and lifestyle that society pushed onto us. Most people are so mentally exhausted and their brains so full of static that to try to contemplate on the deep inner things of one's self is almost an impossibility.

I am so glad that my journey of questioning things began several years ago. I still did not have the brain space to focus on too many things as my brain's "RAM" was completely used up trying to survive. Out of the pain of realizing my life was spiraling out of control, came the positioning and preparedness neces-sary to take advantage of the quiet when it did come. Since I was already comfortable with the idea of questioning my religion and nationalism, when the quietness and calm of the covid shutdown and subsequent loss of my job came around, I was in the perfect place to ask deep questions of myself. Had the shutdown not come around, had I continued in my career as normal, I would probably still be floundering in a system that I knew I didn't belong in, but yet would not have the time, energy, or brain space to change. It is sad that I, in my upper thirties am just now discovering myself in a way that should be a norm for all young adults and even children. By sending our children off to educational institutes so young; by pressuring them into jobs and careers so quickly after education; by society's taking up of all available energy and brain space to prop itself up, ensures that humanity will just continue down a path towards nonexistence. There should be at the least, a prerequisite of two years or so, of travel between high school and further education or career, just to allow our younger generation to discover what truly makes them tick. We would have much more passionate people because then at least they would have had the opportunity to actually figure out what makes them happy. You would not have people pursuing meaningless degrees just for the sake of going to college, without even knowing what they truly want to do. Many end up graduating college and beginning their life with massive debt, and still do not know what career they should pursue. There may be some people forced into construction or any other career, when their passion would truly be space exploration. Without the time or quietness that is required to realize this, we have people pursuing things they don't even like. With colleges being run as a place of business, taking young people's money as fast as they can, and with ridiculous rise in cost, it starts some young adults out in a deficit, rather than giving them the leap forward that they need. It can also keep those who could truly do great things from attaining further education because it is simply too costly to pursue their passions. Education has become more of a franchise than a public service.

CHAPTER 5:

RELIGION

THE TOPIC OF RELIGION IS one of the hardest topics to discuss, especially if any amount of criticism is used during the discussion. I will say this many times throughout this book, that I do not wish to offend anyone, nor do I believe the particular religions that I discuss are worse than others necessarily. Some do tend to be more violent than others, but which is which can be debated. The ones I discuss are simply what I know best, with Christianity being the predominant one. Also, it is very difficult to speak into a family, culture, nation, or religion that you are not a part of. I come from the United States and from Christianity. These are the two areas I focus on because it is what I know and where I believe I can have the most impact. I do not necessarily think any of these two are worse than China, Russia, Britain, Islam, Judaism, Sikhism, etc.... When our nationalism and religion have become so intertwined, it is very difficult to stand back and listen to criticism and not feel attacked.

We also tend to have a worldview dependent on our nationalism and religion that if either one is shaken it feels as though our world is crumbling down. If you can, try to remember that both nationalism and Christianity, in their current form, are both manmade. A good way to test this out is that anything built and constructed by God (according to Christianity) should be unshakeable. I believe this is a core tenant of Christianity. If your view of both nationalism/patriotism and Christianity can be shaken and crumbled, then it was never on a firm foundation and was probably completely manmade. If either view begins to crumble, then consider allowing them to do just that. It may be the best thing that could happen. We also tend to get angry or overly defensive if something speaks to, or contradicts something that we do not want to be challenged. If something that is said makes you defensive or angry, then chances are it is something that needs to be examined. Don't be afraid of this. Take a break if you need to. Take small bites.

Christianity, this is where I come from. It was my crutch for many years. I formed my world views around it. I was taught that the core of my being was corrupted by "The Fall" and could not be trusted. What the implication was is that I should allow Christianity and the Bible to form my morality and world views. The thought was that the Bible is the "Word" of God, living and breathing, given to us to answer all of life's questions. One could form all their political beliefs and world views completely based on the contents of the Bible. All of one's morality could be derived from this book. Have a question about any of it? Look in the book. This book was to be considered inerrant and essentially the Truth with a capital "T". What I have found is that Christianity in and of itself is not a bad thing. Where Christianity (and probably many other religions) fail or "shoots itself in the foot" is actually through, or because of these huge claims of inerrancy and absolute "Truth". These claims are the root cause for many exiting out of the religion. If these types of absolutes are taught about a certain thing such as the bible, then when any small discrepancy is found it calls into question one's whole belief system. The problem isn't the fact that the bible contains contradictions and falls short on moral issues. The problems are the claims that it doesn't and that everything is morally and factually true. If these claims were not made and a different approach were taken, then the problems wouldn't be problems to begin with. What many are doing is doing a critical analysis of these claims and realizing that they fall flat on their face. Furthermore, many of today's religions are being so closely tied to nationalism that it is very hard to tell the two apart.

Christianity is all about exclusivity, which is one of the reasons why it plays into politics so well. I see this when, during a disaster, I see Christians asking other Christians to pray for the Christians effected by the disaster. I always find this so strange. It's as if all they care about are fellow Christians. There will also be examples of great people working tirelessly to provide necessities such as food and shelter to devastated people, and Christians will focus on sharing videos of a group, in the middle of an ongoing disaster, singing praise and worship songs. They talk about how great the Christians are for worshipping and praying "in the midst of the storm" but fail to recognize people placing action behind their words. One atheist willing to physically work to help those in need will always outdo an entire group that prays for relief. I understand that keeping one's spirits up can help you keep your strength up, however this does not take the place of physical actions. I saw this call for prayer specifically for Christians during the Isis disaster in Iraq, and the ongoing one in Ukraine. It's as if some do not even see that the persecution was happening to others as well, or simply don't care about others. It's all about those within the Christian borders. This mentality plays right into placing a nation first, and only really caring about the prosperity of a specific people group. To be fair, I do not believe most of these "exclusive" Christians are intentionally doing this. They are simply so indoctrinated and laser focused that they can't see anything else.

This causes another problem when a person begins to look at the world's population as being one unified people. When one's nationalism is so closely tied to a religion and vice versa, if a person begins to question one it generally leads to questioning the other. If one is used to prop up the other, then one should be prepared to have both crumble if either is called into question. The problem is kind of a Christian problem though because Christianity sort of came into prominence through the adoption of it as a national religion. Sure, Christianity had its start in a much more humble place, but did end up gaining global power through its affiliation with Rome. I personally believe it flourished because it was bent in such a way that it became an excellent religion that could serve government perfectly. Once Christianity gained power, it held onto it and did so vehemently. As a state religion it flourished and did not hesitate to use stately powers to do so. It quickly began persecuting as badly as it had been persecuted. Rome was also ecstatic with this religion because it worked very well to unite the empire behind a common religion. The religion taught obedience to power. It taught that the persons in power were placed there by god for his purposes. The adherents to Christianity were also taught exclusivity through the religion and could thus be taught to look down against anyone deemed and enemy to the church, which quite often ended up being an enemy to the nation as well. As a state religion, the church needed unquestioning power. It required its people to adhere to it unquestioningly and required ultimate submission. This would of course make sense as to why the church began making claims its writings were without error, and were capable of being the ultimate moral authority. The church held such close allegiance to the empire that Rome gave the church great power and even allowed it to have its own police force. The church would round up people that stood in opposition to it and used the government to execute capital punishment. It worked out wonderfully because eventually the church essentially kept all the subjects in line through its own power. I mean what government wouldn't like that? The church however, did eventually just take killing into its own hands. The practice of burning and executing apostates was a common practice all the way up to modern times. Even the protestant movement quickly adopted the practice of executing heretics, even though Protestantism itself was born from a place of being persecuted themselves. Remember the claim I made that Europeans of the time were within systems that would use power in harsh ways once they came to power? The persecuted would quickly become the persecutors. This is a perfect example of this. I say all of this to point out that very shortly after its conception, Christianity quickly sold out to government and power. After that I believe that Christianity has been flawed at its very foundations. It has never fully recovered and continues to exist in its adulterated form.

In my opinion, Christianity could possibly be very relevant if it were able to undo the corruption inflicted on it. I don't know this for sure. It may have come too far and its true origins may be lost forever. As of now Christianity simply fits too closely with government and nationalistic views. A hot topic that we can all relate to and use as an example is something like slavery. I know deep on the inside of me that having a slave is a bad thing. A nation or group can however, call you to bypass your humanity and condone slavery because of what is written in scripture. In modern times, almost two thousand years after the time of Jesus, nations did still condone slavery through the use of the bible. To be fair, we need to look at the context of where and when it was written. This actually has a large impact on the meanings of things. The Bible does not say anything about slavery being a bad thing, it actually tells the slave to be obedient to its master. This of course does not add any brownie points to the bible. Where the bible was revolutionary for its time was in how it instructed slave owners to treat their slaves. The bible forbade slave owners to beat their slaves until they died (Exodus 21:20). You could beat them but not beat them to death. This was a new thing in its day because slaves were totally possessed by the owner who could do whatever he wanted. The bible actually gave a tiny bit of dignity and value to the slave. There were also laws that slaves could be set free after so much time depending on the situation, etc. These teachings were actually counter cultural and helped progress society forward. Today however, if I base my morals on the writings and teachings of the bible, I can totally justify having slaves. This flies flat in the face of the moral compass that we as a society contain within us today. In that way, the bible could be countercultural once again, but not in a good way. It is kind of like attacking in the wrong direction. This is what I mean by using the bible to bypass our morality. We know inside that something is wrong, however if you live only the bible, you can justify committing horrible injustices. This is what the world did for a very long time, long after society knew better. Many of the laws concerning the treatment of slaves in the United States were derived from biblical teachings. This is where Western Christianity fails. It has sold out to power, and really only serves those in a position of power. I am aware of Christians in other nations that are facing real persecution and I am not talking to that. Christianity in those situations can be used as a real source of comfort and peace. In that context, Christianity should have been used to bring whatever comfort that it could to the American slaves. It could have given them a way to mourn. It could have given a voice to their oppression. It could have been a source of comfort and peace. Instead, it was a way of bringing them into submission. It was just a tool that was used to keep the privileged in power and the weak in submission. It was used in its complete opposite intended form. In such a way, as a voice to the oppressed, Christianity would probably be closely related to its true intended form. I just think that when Christians in America cry persecution because we have separation of church and state, they actually exemplify the very problem within Western Christianity. It goes to prove that our version of Christianity has no power in their lives, or anyone else's unless it is seated in a place of power such as marriage with a government. It has very little spiritual or inner healing power derived from within itself. It has very little power to enact change within a person. Today in America, Christianity really only has power when it is given power by the government. Otherwise, it has become very weak and flaccid. Christianity is more of a political statement than anything else.

Christians must realize that the Bible was written to a specific audience at a specific time and was a very revolutionary item in its day. I can still get wisdom and very valuable things from the Bible, however I can no longer set my moral compass completely on the teachings of the Bible. There is great literature and heartfelt grief that is expressed by people in exile. Many of its beautiful writings come from a place of brokenness and mourning. These people who wrote this stuff were writing from a serious place of oppression. If these writings are used in that context and are used as a tool to help one through similar situations then it can be a wonderful thing. Unfortunately today we use it mostly to leverage power and force our wills upon others. The early Christians also took a massive step forward in how they treated unwanted children. Christians did not believe in infanticide. Christians did not set their unwanted babies (normally female babies) outside in the elements to die of exposure like other cultures did around them. In short, early Christians and Jews began some great social reformations. In their day they truly were the good moral example in some things, but not necessarily today. Female babies were still not as valuable as male babies, but at least they weren't killing them in such grotesque ways simply because they didn't want another mouth to feed or because they did not want the responsibility of finding a husband for them. This did not completely resolve the problem, however it was a step forward. If we could see this and use it appropriately then Christianity could still be on the forefront of reformation. If Christianity could see that it, at its foundations was adapted to its culture to stand in opposition to the systems that were being so unjust to others, it could still do the same today. Something that many people who are trying to attack the bible do is bring up issues such as how Israelites treated captured young girls during their conquest (and this is a valid argument). You must however keep it in its context. Now I will forewarn that this is very disturbing and sickening and I am in no way condoning their actions, but once again try to see the advancement. In the ancient days of Israel, when an army conquered a land or city, it was acceptable to kill everyone, rape the women, especially young virgins of the conquered people, and then dispatch them when they were done with them, right there on the spot. They could keep them as sex slaves if they wanted, but didn't need to. You could also take them as a wife, albeit normally more of a concubine, however many of them just killed the females on the spot after they were done with them. Deuteronomy 21:10-14 in The Old Testament told the Israelites to take them home and not kill them right away. Give them time to mourn before making them your "wife". Now we know that "making them their wife" is a palatable way the biblical writers wrote "rape". If you were still unsatisfied and no longer wanted them after their "trial period" then you could release them out into the wilderness essentially. Abraham did this with Ishmael and Hagar. Now this still sounds very grotesque to us, and rightfully so, but it was revolutionary in its day. It did keep the warriors from potentially acting from the adrenaline of the moment and in turn, give them time to think from a rational and more compassionate mind. It did spare the lives of some and if released into the wilderness they may still have some kind of a chance, or at least keep their conscience somewhat clean by knowing they didn't kill them with their hands. It tried to get them to treat them somewhat decently FOR THEIR TIME AND CULTURE. So once again, for its day these writings were advanced and helped society move forward, but falls flat on its face if I attempt to set my moral compass by it today. Please get what I am saying. I am not saying that their actions and morals are justified, because they are not. It's simply there to point out to both sides that Christianity did some things at least halfway right back in the day, but does little to help us today.

Given the examples above, we can see that almost no one today would consider the so-called revolutionary ideas of that time as even being close to moral today. Islam in its moral standings is just as bad if not worse. Islam continues to struggle in a more archaic fashion among super conservative sects of the religion. I do know that some conservative forms of Christianity in America such as Amish and Mennonite traditions are still very rudimentary in their treatment of females to this day. They may not still be practicing the act of beheading like Islam still does, but the sexual immorality still runs rampant, and the rape of females and boys is still fairly common. Some may kick back at this, but when you look into the dark closets of the anabaptists in this country, you find many scary skeletons there. From the outside, some of the "plain people" religions look so quaint and well composed from the outside. Children are so well behaved, and women stick by their husband's sides like glue. What people do not see is the internal fear and manipulation used to keep it that way. The physical and sexual abuse is shocking. Males in these conservative religions still wield ultimate power, which is a breeding ground for any narcissistic male or any man with the thirst for power. Many men with evil intentions thrive in such environments, and this has proven true ever since religions have become organized and run as institutions. In these cases, religion does not heal a person with evil intentions, but rather exacerbates it. Judaism went through a horrible dark period as well. Afterall it is the foundational religion of the two bloodiest religions in existence, Christianity, and Islam. The saving grace for Judaism is its adaptability to a progressing culture. You can even see this progression through the tainted version of the Hebrew bible that Christianity possesses. Judaism progressed from multi-theism to monotheism, from child sacrifice to outright denouncing it. I am sure it still has its dark sides, however many Jews have come to read their texts in a more loose way, gaining wisdom from it rather than reading it in such a literal and historical way. This may also come by realizing some of the claims made in their writings are too fantastical to be real, and they can see the archaeological evidence in their own country that disproves some of the stories. Judaism may also realize that it would be responsible for the most heinous actions in history if some stories were taken literally. Many Christians, Jews and Muslims are realizing that a literal and historical reading of their texts just simply will not suffice in modern culture. This is why setting your moral standards on the teachings of the Bible, or any religion, can actually be counter cultural today. If we attempt to use these scriptures and apply them today, it will restrict cultural progress and hinder the evolution of the world. An example of how the law in Deuteronomy 21 was used in a very grotesque way is in Numbers 31 when the Israelites fought the Midianites. In this account the Israelites slaughtered all the fighting age males of Midian but kept all the women and their children. They spared them and brought them back to their camp as slaves. This angered Moses who told them they could only keep the virgin girls who never "knew a man". This would have been a direct reflection of the law in Deuteronomy. He ordered them to slaughter all the women and male babies, which were in the tens if not hundreds of thousands according to the story. He did this to not anger God. Could you imagine the horrendous scene if you were to watch this slaughter? Thirty-two thousand left over women who had not "known a man" that were young virgin girls probably fourteen or younger were spared, and the Israelite men could literally have their way with them. Now thirty-two of these virgins were to be set aside for the Levites as a "tribute" and "offering to the Lord". Think about this for a minute. This either means they were sacrificed to God, used as sex slaves by the Levites or sold as sex slaves by the Levites. The "priests of the Lord" taking part in sex trafficking, all in the name of "God" at that. That should get anyone's attention and raise serious concerns here. As a side note, Christianity may want to reconsider how "literally true" every jot and tittle of this book is. If this is actually taught as absolute truth, it makes God, more specifically Yahweh, out to be a monster. There is no way around that fact and many people in current generations are seeing this and have absolutely no desire to serve such a god. They rightfully place these stories, along with this god, in the category of a mythicized deity, right next to the Iliad and the Odyssey, and leave it alone. This angers Christians and they blame the world for denying God, all the time not realizing their literal interpretation of the bible is the exact thing that is driving everyone away. Christians are Christianity's own worst enemy, not the devil. Now to be honest, this may actually be a hidden blessing for the world, because quite frankly, I believe the world would be a much less bloody place without these top three Abrahamic religions. God (Yahweh) quite literally has a higher kill count than any other deity in history, even outdoing Satan by quite a bit. In the Old Testament alone, god is credited with killing people in the millions with the devil being accredited for about ten. Even worse, I don't think god's killing efficiency even counts the flood and it does not count women and children. Of course it doesn't, because throughout the Hebrew bible, women and children simply don't count at all. According to some, Yahweh's kill count is still rising, because apparently the invasion of Ukraine is the will of God. It is claimed that God is taking out evil governments through Putin and his armies. This once again makes Yahweh out to be a monster and a weakling who can only have his will accomplished through the killing of innocent people. The soldiers, civilians, and children had nothing to do with either government, but continually seem to be the ones who pay in blood for the sins of their nations. Why could god not take action in some other way, against the people actually responsible? This is once again a version of human blood sacrifice, which leads to the conclusion that the "cross" meant nothing either. If it did, then Yahweh would not require the death or blood of any single human or animal to ever be spilt again. Why could god not be the one in the subway tunnels, in the trenches with the soldiers, giving calm and peace to the ones caught in the middle of evil nation's games? But no, to some American Christians, Jesus is driving one of the tanks, or guiding one of the bombs. Christianity and its founding religion are full of blood magic and stories, if written anywhere else, would never in anyone's wildest dreams be considered true. One such story in Exodus 4 tells the story of Moses' return trip to Egypt. He is literally doing as the "Lord" commands him. It says that when Moses was on the way to camp that the "Lord met him and tried to kill him." Zipporah, Moses' wife "took a flint and cut off her son's foreskin, and touched Moses' feet (probably meaning groin) with it." She says "Truly you are a bridegroom of blood to me!" So god leaves Moses alone and all is well. The end... What?!? There are still people saying this stuff is factually true! Furthermore,

Moses and Zipporah would have went directly against the will of God (because God was trying to kill him after all) and used some sort of blood magic to overcome God. This is insanity.

How about the New Testament God? Does he vindicate himself through his portrayal as a kind affectionate god? No he does not. We are taught that god is unchanging, and yet there is a clear changing of the heart of god between the two books. Although this is contradictory to some Christians still saying he does the things in places like Ukraine to get his will accomplished. To say that god really doesn't change but rather sees us through the sacrifice of Jesus does not help the case at all. This would mean that god still wants to kill me, but Jesus somehow talks him out of it. It seems that Jesus fails from time to time, and god still gets his fix though when he can kill people in Ukraine, Iraq, Somalia, and Syria. It still would take the blood human sacrifice to appease this god in order for him to be able to just look at me. To make sure that we all can see that Christianity still definitely looks at god as the same vengeful god, we can look at some songs and literature. There is a Christian singer (whom I actually like very much) that sings a song something like this, "I am guilty, ashamed of what I've done, what I've become, these hands are dirty, I dare not lift them up to the Holy One". Now I get the mentality here. I was a Christian for many years. The whole connotation behind this is still of an angry vengeful god whom we do not even deserve to look at. The only way this is possible is because there had to be a human killed in a very horrific way in order for him to even somewhat accept us. Even still Revelation 6:16 makes it very clear that this is only temporary and god will still have his grand finale, coming back to slaughter billions of people who have not bent the knee to him. This book is full of passages like "every slave, every free man, hid themselves in the caves and in the rocks of the mountains, and said to the mountains and rocks, 'Fall on us and hide us from the face of Him who sits on the throne and from the wrath of the Lamb! For the day of His wrath has come'" Rev 6:16. There is also supposed to be blood running down the streets about four feet deep or the height of the "horse's bridal". Christianity brags about this stuff as if it is a wonderful thing! I heard two Christians conversing recently and using these scriptures as a "you wait and see" type of justification that will happen. Christianity is obsessed with blood, murder, and sacrifice and this still isn't enough to keep this god from wiping out most of the very things he created, including the planets and stars. Can you blame anyone from running away from that religion? I can't. I don't want anything to do with a god like that either. He makes Zeus and Baal look like a teddy bear. As much as Christianity claims that Islam is a bloodthirsty and scary religion, they way out do Islam in their blood thirst and body counts. This is also evident in the death counts of the Christian religion. Christianity has been used as a reasoning tool to justify the killing of millions upon millions of people throughout history. We still use it, including the United States, for that reason to this day. We have a hard time staying out of a war for more than ten years. We just ended a twenty year war and already we are staring down one of the other superpowers of the world, threatening the use of force around every corner. We are a nation of peace, and we'll destroy as many other nations as we need to keep it too. The EU and many of its members are guilty too. As a matter of fact, all major and even most minor governments are guilty. This is once again the Janus faced propaganda we are so good at. We say we want peace, but really, we just want to ensure our safety in the states. We wreak havoc on any other nation as long as we can live in comfort. Sorry, I'm going off on a tangent, but this stuff makes my blood boil.

Some would still say that the Bible's teachings of being faithful to your spouse and to not murder another human is a good thing. These are true however, if the only thing keeping you from treating another person in a horrible manner is the teachings of the bible or any other writings. If this is true, then you have serious issues that need to be resolved. In other words, if you do not go out and murder someone only because the bible tells you not to then you have a serious problem. Please find help now! I mean seriously, do not finish reading this book. Put it down now and call a professional. The truth of the matter is that if something such as murder and unfaithfulness is something that is honestly a desire of your heart, then the time will come when you will do it anyway. No law or teaching will ever keep you from committing something that is already in your heart. Your heart must be set on good and wholesome things first, then if you must, use religion to add deeper meaning. In places such as Afghanistan and other strict cultures and religions, a person can still be beheaded for being unfaithful to a spouse. This still doesn't stop people from doing it. No law can ever be a substitute for morality. In some cultures, hands were cut off for stealing, and yet there were thieves. This is what we have lost sight of. Is it a good thing to have a law that says you cannot murder someone in cold blood? Yes it is. Does it stop someone with murder in their heart? No. So why is it good to have that law? It merely gives authority to the law enforcers to hold someone accountable. It simply gives authority and the ability to properly address the situation, but not to prevent it from happening. If there were no law to the contrary, then the authorities would have no power to take the appropriate actions. We have lost sight of the reasons for laws and spirituality in this world. We continually want to legislate morality into our society, and most are completely ignorant to the fact that it will never work. The prohibition of alcohol and drugs is proof to that. We have made both illegal and neither one solved the problem. In fact it may have exacerbated the problem. If something is made illegal but a demand still remains, it leaves a power or supply vacuum, maybe both. During prohibition people still demanded alcohol which took alcohol from a publicly traded good in the "light", and moved it to a dark underbelly of society that gave room for mobsters and organized violence on a scale never before seen in America. Anytime you move something from light to darkness by placing shame, doubt, guilt, or any similar trait to anything, it still continues to thrive, but in a more hurtful way. Many conservative religious groups place shame on sex and masturbation, so it just moves to molestation, rape, and pornography addictions. This same problem still exists in America when applied to the subject of drugs. Many people addicted to medically prescribed opioids remain somewhat functional and take place in society the way anyone else does. A "drug addict" addicted to street drugs will normally regress and shy away from society. The person addicted to street drugs is no worse, this person is only recognizing the darkness attached to the drugs he/she takes. I knew just as many, if not more, people addicted to prescription drugs than I did people addicted to street drugs. Only the ones addicted to street drugs had to deal with the shame that society placed on them. Most people on prescription drugs do not have the fear of prison either. Even Christianity has this thing with bringing things out of the darkness and into the light, not the other way around. I'm not even talking about bringing someone's addiction into the light. Simply stop placing shame and guilt on them. Accept them into your circles and treat them the same as anyone else. This would be a much mor successful "war on drugs" than what we have now. If abortion is ever made illegal, it will be applicable there too. I recently looked into the abortion laws of this country. It turns out that many conservatives and Christians are lying about those too. I'm not taking a stance on right or wrong when it comes to this subject. I'm just saying that Christians will lie or bend the truth as quick as anybody in order to get their way. Murder, violence, theft, and all sorts of things have been prohibited from the dawn of society and there is still plenty of it happening. Laws do not stop anything from happening. Never have, never will.

I am of the belief that goodness and morality reside on the inside of every human. This goodness may have been covered or obscured due to life events, but they are still there. I believe we as humans need to dig deeper into the core of who we truly are, not shy away from it. We need to stop teaching our children that they are inherently defiled and bad. They need to hear that they are inherently good, and the right answer can be found within them. We need to take people who have been hurt and who are in pain, and teach them that there is goodness within them. We do not need to introduce hurting people to the band aid of religion as an answer to their problem. Religion is part of the problem. Religion is the very thing that creates the idea within one's self that you are evil, and then offers the medicine to fix it. The Inherent goodness within them needs to be found first, then if they want to supplement with religion (a healthy one) they can. People are not born evil. Babies are not evil. Something has to creep in first. If you attempt to bring in religion first, then it normally gets used as a cover that buries the true problems. Why do we not work on creating a society that does not damage its children? When something inevitably does cause pain to a young one, why do we not teach them how to heal from it. Many children in the anabaptist community that get assaulted can't even talk about it. Often the victims are punished and spanked for bringing up anything on the subject of sex, even if it is about their own assault. Sex is such a shameful thing in these communities that a person cannot even turn their abuser or talk about the event. Thankfully I was never assaulted in this way, but I know many that were. I absolutely cannot imagine being punished for trying to talk about such a traumatic event, while the abuser walks free and un-punished.

For me, I had many unresolved issues (as many young adults do) that I was taught could be prayed away or that simply don't exist after one becomes a Christian. This was very untrue. These teachings kept sweeping my problems under the rug and left them largely unresolved. I had serious issues and remained in a lot of pain. For years because I kept praying and waiting for God to resolve my problems. I only made any significant progress after I realized that my religion wasn't going to solve my issues. Once I quit praying them away and actually addressed my issues face-to-face, I finally made a lot of headway. If you keep praying and going to meetings to get some sort of relief, but yet keep running into the same issues down the road then you need to realize that you are only acquiring temporary reprieve from your issues and not actually ridding yourself from them. Can religion help by giving you a temporary relief from emotional pain? Yes, it can, but it should only be used as such to keep your nose above water, sane, or alive until the issues can be addressed properly. A life jacket or a life raft were never intended to become permanent floatation devices. They are merely meant to last long enough for one to get rescued by a ship or until you can reach dry land. Religion should be used in a similar fashion, if it must be used at all. Religion such as Christianity can be used to help rescue people momentarily, but rarely serve as the permanent solution to the problems. This isn't a criticism of Christianity alone. I believe this to be true with all forms of spirituality. Even if you are into more modern types of spirituality in all of its forms, I believe that personal progress and the solution to inward problems still only comes, in large, by intentional and focused work. Meditation is a very useful thing, and it can help you remain centered, but it should help you remain centered in your endeavor of self-improvement. It may give you clarity to deal with things, but it will never deal with things FOR you or in place of you. Most of the time you can only deal with real pain and trauma through the dirty work of getting down into the trenches and facing your issues head-on. I have found much peace and help in my spiritual practices, but none of it, past or present, makes my issues magically disappear. There is no easy way out! No religion or god will come down and take all your pain away. Some religion or spirituality can offer comfort for a time, but should not, in my experience, be used as a permanent solution. You deserve to be free from the trauma that you suffered in your life, and no religion or spirituality will magically whisp them away. I would hate to see loved ones, struggle with pain that has been vexing them since childhood, go to the end of their life, waiting on god to take it all away. Sadly, many do this. I see it everywhere. People need to know that there is healing. The healing is inside of you. You need to participate in it in order to bring it to fruition. I believe we need to go back to using religion and spirituality as a tool to help us in our journey and not depend on it to do the walking for us.

I believe Christianity has reached a place or level of existence that it was never intended to be at. Even though I am just kind of done with the religion, I personally believe that Christianity was started not even so much as an organization or system to reach heaven, but as a lifestyle or "way" that a person could follow to gain enlightenment. Think about it. What time did these Israelites live in? They lived in a horribly oppressive time under the horrible domineering nation of Rome. I believe the founder, its namesake, never intended it to be an organized system of denominations that was meant to gain access to a physical "heaven" and to escape an eternal damnation. I believe he was attempting to help his distraught followers find a way to live above the systems of oppression. To be able to thrive regardless of the chaos around them. Regardless of the original intent of Christ, there were well intentioned and loving followers who, little by little, trying to protect their "way" or beliefs, trying to make it work among a very systematic world, started adding structures and systems to their beliefs. Eventually the belief that others need to think and act as I do in order for it to work settled in. Over time, I believe, there were some ill-intentioned people who added to this for their own gain and for the gain of governments and churches. I am no scholar and do not wish to make any super deep scholarly claims, however I believe that some of this outside influence can be traced back to some of the great "patriarchal fathers" of the church. Many of these early patriarchs were highly bigoted and sexist. I believe many of these patriarchs were influenced through politics and corrupt personal viewpoints and agendas, going as far as adding to and subtracting from original scripture. It eventually ended up in its predominant current form as a thing that requires people to live how they are told in order to escape eternal torture and damnation. Our current social systems may well be a product of the same sort. I believe most religions that survived until today are the ones that could easily be manipulated into a tool to promote nations. They are used to unify nations behind ideologies. They are used to demonize or vilify other people. They are used to justify wars and all sorts of horrible actions. You can easily teach the hatred of others through many of todays religions. Most of these religions would even profess to be religions of love and acceptance. Most are still tied to the archaic notion that a certain god gives favor to whatever people or nation that is willing to pay homage to it. There is a very ancient notion that the nation who appeases their god more will be victorious in battle. There are Christians praying to Yahweh in bot Ukraine and Russia, in both Iraq and America. The nation who obeys the commandments of their god the best will be the favored ones. We would pray to the same god that Russia prays to, but obviously they are of the wrong denomination. They serve the Eastern Orthodox church, which is undoubtedly heretical (I say this in jest of course). Even the ancient Israelites gave credit to this notion of appeasing gods when King Mesha sacrificed his son on the city walls (2Kings 3:27). Israel was coming against King Mesha and the Moabites. The Israelites were laying waste to the Moabites until King Mesha sacrificed his son on the city walls. This granted him some special power from his god allowing him to drive back the Israelites. End of story. No further explanation. This would imply that in the "war of the gods" that there was for one, more than one god, and that this act gave this other god more power than Yahweh and enabled the Moabites to drive back the Israelites. Apparently,

Yahweh isn't all powerful. Apparently, you can circumcise your kid to overcome him when he tries to kill you and you can sacrifice your son if you want to defeat him in battle. A little food for thought for modern Christians. My point to this is that religion including Christianity has been used time and time again by many different nations to unify a people group behind a common cause, even warfare. Europeans most definitely used Christianity to justify the slaughter of the native peoples of the Americas. Americans used Christianity to justify slavery. The United States even used biblical rules for slavery to outline the treatment of their slaves, which was very grotesque. When we went to war after 9/11, one of the first things our president did was bring in a Christian pastor to unify our nation and to call for God's blessing on our nation as we wage war on our enemies. Once again this is not some political statement. I am simply pointing out that Christianity is the driving force that we use to unite our nation, even if it is for a horrible cause. We also hang onto the ancient ideology of the god of the universe somehow being more partial to our nation and our people, giving us special treatment, thereby enabling us to kill more of them than us. In short, I believe that religion in general has made some very major blunders throughout our human history. Many have sold out to nations in order to gain power and prominence. Christianity was a fringe off chute of Judaism and was having a hard go of it. Christianity had the opportunity to become an acceptable and powerful religion under the Roman empire. The problem with this is that even though it gave Christianity major power, it also had to pay homage to government at the same time. A religion normally does not become a national religion if the government cannot benefit from it. Afterall, Constantine used Christianity only after he believed it gave him victory in battle. Christianity needed to be bent and twisted so that it could be used by the empire to justify the ruling of people by a king and to unite the empire against a common enemy. Christianity worked so well at this that it ultimately became the national religion of many nations throughout history and was used in the bloodiest "holy war" of all time. Read up on the Crusades and the witch hunts that followed. Even though Hitler did not necessarily profess to be Christian, his "PR guy" Joseph Goebbels used Christianity to unite Germany and the Nazi party in order to justify the extermination of the Jews. Fourteen million lives were lost in this single conflict. Even today in the United States, if you want to run for president in the conservative wing of government then professing to be Christian is basically a pre-requisite.

CHAPTER 6:

RELIGION PART 2

MY APOLOGIES FOR HARPING ON religion so much. I simply feel that so much of our society has been driven and established by religion and its views. A whole book could be dedicated to this subject, which probably has been done. Even for a book that isn't trying to get into any one subject too deeply, the subject cannot adequately be covered in just one chapter.

If religion has become something so far removed from what it should be, is it still salvageable? I don't think that is an easy question to answer. I believe many previous religions found their demise in either being driven out by more aggressive religions, or they were making claims that eventually could not be upheld. When religions make great claims and make absolute statements, eventually the people under these religions begin to ask questions. If the claims of the religion cannot withstand scrutiny, then eventually it will kind of fizzle out. I think this is true of many cultural ideas and trends, not just religion. This was essentially the reason or at least the cata-lyst that moved me away from the Christian religion. This is due to the fact that most religions depend on ignorance and unquestion-able authority. A person or system of authority also needs access to something higher than themselves to provide answers and powers to its subjects. Have a drought? "Let me summon the gods and inquire why this drought happened. We were not pleasing to the gods. I can reverse this for you, but it will require a ritual that only I have access to in order to reverse it." Need victory in battle? "My god can provide it." This was a typical starting point of many ancient religions. If they had special powers or access that the commoners did not, it gave a concrete reason for them to remain in power.

I was taught throughout my Christian life of the absolute authority of the Bible. I was taught every "jot and tittle" of the book was God's inerrant and living word. I was taught that Christianity alone held the answer to salvation and a good life here on earth. I was also taught that the Christian god was the only real god in the universe and only he could grant salvation and an eternal life in heaven. This salvation came through the belief in his son Jesus, who was god as well, yet somehow not fully god, who was also fully human, yet also fully divine too… somehow. That's not to mention the third person of a "Trinity", the spirit who was also separate but also fully god and divine as well, but different… somehow. I know to Christians this sounds as though I may be poking fun, but I'm not. Just hang in there a bit. This really is the mental gymnastics that it takes, unless you just turn a blind eye and don't think of them at all. The thing of it is that I simply began asking basic questions about things I found in the Bible. I had found huge audacious claims and discrepancies in the Bible. I would have questions such as, "If God is all powerful and all loving, why did he just resort to killing people that he had a problem with?" This seemed to me like an easy or "cheep" way out of a problem. I think being diplomatic and reasonable is the tougher and higher road. Afterall, this is why most nations go to war. It is usually easier to fight it out than it is to find a diplomatic answer. I was called to love my enemies and God could just kill His enemies. It honestly seemed to me that God raised the bar for me and required me to display more morality and compassion than He did. It felt like humanity had to leap over huge hurdles and jump through hoops, and yet we lowered the bars for God so he could gingerly step over them. I am the curious type so I would ask church leaders about these questions. I would ask people I looked up to who seemed to be very knowledgeable about all things Christian. I quite literally did what I thought I should and ask the ones who should have the answers. I seriously thought they would have answers. They didn't. I mean quite literally, they had no answers. These are serious questions that in all honesty should have some very good and deep answers. You would think that Christianity, after at least fifteen hundred years would have developed some creative answers to this. The reason is that most of church history required unquestionable allegiance. It didn't need answers if no one could ask. Most of the time I received answers that were somehow glazed over and almost never gave any satisfying answers. I don't mean that it didn't give answers that made me feel good. I mean it gave no answers with any substance, often giving little to no answer at all. I would say that at least half the time the answer was something like "God works in mysterious ways. We may never know the real answers in this life. We just know that His ways are higher than our ways." These types of answers were normally followed with an exhortation to stay faithful and simply trust God. These answers simply were not good enough after a while. I began looking into these things for myself. I had to. No one else seemed to know, and I am the type that can only remain curious so long. The answers burned inside me and no one was able to extinguish them. I would also have questions such as how the story of Noah's ark was possible. I am no scientist or physicist, but some things seemed a little tough to explain. I could literally write a couple chapters on the problems with the story, however my basic questions will need to suffice for now. Aside from the mass genocide, I would question how could a flood of such magnitude happen in only forty days and nights? I mean to cover the whole earth along with its mountains in that amount of time would require such a deluge of water that it would destroy the very ark that was meant to save Noah! The waters would have to rise nearly thirty-one feet (9.4 meters) per hour continuously for a month and a half to achieve such a flood. The inflow of water on such a scale would rip everything apart including the ark. What about the massive tidal waves? The rain alone would probably rip apart our very atmosphere for that matter. Have you ever noticed the rush of air leading a heavy rainstorm? The wind blows fairly strong sometimes for about ten minutes prior to the rain falling. Now mind you, this was just my mind randomly thinking about this stuff. The things I would lay awake thinking about because my mind just works this way. A rain drop falling to earth needs to displace the atmosphere around it. The air and a raindrop cannot occupy the same space at the same time. One of them needs to move. During a heavy rainstorm you would have, what I presume to be tens of thousands of raindrops falling simultaneously, displacing the atmosphere or air that is in its way. This would force a large amount of air to move outside of the storm causing the wind before a heavy rain. This is my thinking on it anyway. Check out the science to see if I'm right, but this is how my brain envisions this. In order for the water that caused Noah's flood to occupy the earth's atmosphere all at once across the whole earth, I would imagine such a massive global wind that it too would have probably destroyed everything in its wake. I would assume that it would have changed atmospheric pressures so much that it would have probably either collapsed or exploded every lung on the planet, killing everything, including Noah, almost instantly. The weight of all this water would have quite literally crushed the earth itself. The heat from all of this would have boiled all of the earth's water.

What about the boat itself? The ark made out of wood could float, technically. Wooden boats smaller than the ark were very hard to keep afloat and required mechanical bilge pumps and crews much larger than eight and still proved difficult. Even the "Arc Exhibit" built in modern times uses steel to keep the structure from collapsing, and it sits on dry land. A fresh wooden boat of that size would spring many leaks on day one of the one year voyage, just from the flexing caused by waves. Waves on the scale of massive tidal waves would have been sure to bombard this ship and break it to pieces. Bailing water out of the ship just from the leaks would have been impossible, let alone the massive amounts of water inundating the vessel from every side for forty days straight. Throw in caring for the animals on top of all this. Would the ark have had room for the animals? Possibly if you only took a pair of each "kind" of species instead of a pair of every living creature. An example would be to only taking a pair of foxes instead of a pair of the whole K-9 species. Also, no dinosaurs, at least not adult ones.

Also, you would not take anything that does not breath through nostrils such as some insects or anything that breaths through its skin. Because it clearly says "all that have breath in their nostrils." Yeah, right. Also, it would largely depend on whether they only had to take two pair or seven pair of the "clean" animals. There are a lot of loopholes for the biblical literalist to jump through apparently. This only attempts to answer the question regarding the animals though. What about food? There would have been no food for them. There would not have been nearly enough room. Water? Well, they definitely could've just drank out of the bottom of the boat. Even if there was room for food and the ark would not have sunk, how could eight people take care of the largest zoo in the world? Imagine the tons upon tons of manure and filth that would have needed dealing with every single day. The rain only lasted forty days, however they were in the ark for about a year. What about plants? There would've been no olive tree for the dove to find. No plants would have survived even a month under saline water. What would the herbivores have eaten after disembarking? Would Noah and his family have eaten the very animals that survived on the ark? What about the carnivorous animals? What would they have eaten? How did whole cities spring up across the land so shortly after the flood? Did Noah's family just pop babies out every single day? What about incest? How did so many species of animals evolve out of so few in such a short amount of time? I know. I am going on a rant here, but I want you to see how my mind works and the serious questions I would have about things. God would have had to pull so many miracles out of his sleeves to make this happen. Why would he not simply snap his fingers and just make it happen? What about the beginning of the story and other instances through the Bible where

God grieves or regrets ever creating humans? What does this say about God? Was He an all loving, all knowing, omnipotent god or not? You cannot regret making humans and be an all knowing god all at the same time. You cannot commit genocide and be all loving. The thing that needs pointed out is that I probably wouldn't have had these questions if the Christian community had never made these bold claims of unquestionable truth and power.

Take the Garden of Eden as another example. Please stick with me here, I'll wrap everything up shortly. God created Adam and Eve to tend to and guard the garden. What were they supposed to guard it against for one? Supposedly there was no evil yet. But not just that, God asked them to not eat from the tree of the knowledge of good and evil. He didn't really explain a whole lot other than saying it would kill them. He never gave the long term implications of damning the whole of creation. I would think it would only be fair to give full disclosure on such a serious consequence. I mean we are talking about sickness, disease, war, famine, drought, floods, and death on a scale they could not comprehend. If He would have disclosed this information could Adam and Eve have "opted out" if they felt the responsibility was too great? Would they have had free will or not? This is still not my main point. Think about what I said earlier, they were commanded to not eat of the tree of the knowledge of good and evil. Following this logic, He commanded them to not disobey Him before they even knew what disobedience was. How could they know they were doing something wrong or evil if they had no idea of what was good or evil. They had absolutely no way of knowing according to the words of this very story. Even when he said they would die, they technically had absolutely no way of knowing whether death itself, was a good or bad thing. They probably wouldn't have even known what death was! Along with giving full disclosure to them prior to giving them this responsibility, I would only consider it fair only if they would have been given the ability to actually grasp the consequences of their disobedience, and given the chance to opt out if they wanted to. Even then it would be questionable. The whole thing that blows my mind with this is that under these circumstances, God himself would have quite literally stacked the deck against humanity and intended to bring damnation onto humanity from the beginning. There is no other logic to this. This would have been the plan from the very beginning. This would have been very dishonest of God, and in fact He would have been the evil one in this story. The serpent would have actually been the upstanding one, because he at least told them the truth. God told them they would die the very day they ate of the tree. They didn't. The serpent told them their eyes would be opened and they would be like gods. It happened. Their eyes were opened and they did become like gods. God himself says this and drives them out of the garden because of his fear of this. In this instance, the serpent was more truthful than God himself. God didn't them out of the garden to spare humanity, but rather to spare himself from the implications of what happened. He had competition if they still ate from the tree of life and became immortal. He was trying to save his own backside. Also when God says "they have become like us" (Genesis 3:22), who was He talking to? Clearly, He was talking to other gods. That's another thing you find out when digging into all this. The people of Israel believed in multiple gods during the time this story was told. You will also find that the story of gardeners in charge of orchards, very similar flood stories and such were found in other cultures around them and even written prior to the ones in

Genesis. Y'all, we have all of these questions without answers, and we haven't even made it to chapter 10 of Genesis.

The problem with all of this is the very stance that Christianity takes on these stories. The fact that they are taught as an unquestionable absolute truth is the very reason why there can be no real explanation of them. Many of these discrepancies in the bible are not that huge, until you claim there are no discrepancies. The very claim that everything is factual and without error is the very thing that makes it a big deal. Judaism quite often (the foundational religion of Christianity) does not make literal claims about many of these stories. Of course some do, but a lot don't. I would say that if there would have been a more relaxed view of the Bible and the writings in it, I would have gained more use out of it. I would have probably had more answers to problems and would have actually been able to use some of the knowledge contained in it to deal with problems that plagued me. Because the common insight on the biblical writings have taken on a more narrow minded version of itself then what I feel it could have, it has forfeited the power, wisdom, and art that it could have. If Christian believers were honest with the biblical writings, and take the approach that these were people like you and I, struggling to understand themselves and the world around them, we could have a much more coherent faith. They were trying to figure out why humans seemed to have higher intelligence and reasoning than the animals around them. How did this great creation come to be? What happens after we die? They were immersed in an oral tradition that was attempting to pass down wisdom from one generation to the next. They had a limited knowledge of science and cosmology. They were attempting to educate and make sense of things the best they could. If you could take the creation story to teach children that god entered into his own creation, breathed himself/herself into each and every one of us. This would infer that divinity was contained within each and every human. This would make every human a sacred creature, pure and holy, a temple worthy of the divine spark we all contain. This would also imply that all of nature contains this same divine essence. It would teach our children that nature is to be cherished and taken care of the way a gardener cares for his orchard. Even though many of the moral standards in the biblical writings fall way short of the morals we have today, we could still see how they were trying to take steps forward. We could see how they were attempting to rise above the crazy injustices taking place around them. We could also see how in their day, the explanation to lightning, thunder, earthquakes, floods, drought, famine, etc. was always to be an act of the gods. The cultures were also pitting their gods against the gods of other cultures. They were attempting to make their gods more powerful and simply better than the ones around them. The Israelites were no different. Having a literal understanding of the scriptures in general is missing out on the creativeness of these ancient writers and story tellers. Instead of their god destroying humanity with a flood because he was simply angry and annoyed at them (like other older flood myths), Yahweh had to destroy humanity because of their evil hearts and the rampant injustices because of it. Instead of a human outsmarting the gods and surviving the flood on a boat (like a competing flood myth), Yahweh chose a family to be spared. This in their eyes made him more powerful and more loving and more knowledgeable. Yahweh was too smart and all knowing to be outsmarted. This same mentality can be continued into the "New Testament" as well. If we could see that when Jesus told "the seventy" in Luke 10 that he saw Satan fall as lightning from the heavens, that this was teaching and making a clear separation between good and evil. People of that day believed that curses, sickness and death were all attributes of God. People believed that Satan was Gods right hand man, doing the will of God. Satan could not act unless given direct permission by God. This can easily be seen in the story of Job. Satan could even be used to test people's faithfulness according to Job. Essentially if you were to take Job's story literally, Job would have suffered unthinkable pain because Yahweh and Satan made a bet. Do you really want to give God such narcissistic attributes? Jesus was making clear that if the forces of darkness were subject to "the seventy" then they clearly could not have the power of God behind them. He was not saying that this was the moment Satan was thrown down from heaven, but rather that these dark things in the world never came from God to begin with, even the ones attributed to Him in the Old Testament. The satanic element of god was symbolically detached and fell from heaven (the realm of the gods). How could they be attached to God in the Old Testament and yet not attached to God during the life of Jesus? Jesus was still living in the Old Testament. Supposedly according to Christianity, nothing should have changed until after the death of Jesus. I believe Jesus was trying to show people a path to enlightenment by bringing out the divinity in us all. He was attempting to show people how to live a more free life by showing them how to think. He was disassociating darkness from light. He was detaching evil from God. Jesus was casting the "Satan" out of the divine realm and disassociating darkness from curses. You can see this in John 9 when Jesus was asked about a blind man. His disciples asked, "who sinned, this man or his parents, that he was born blind?" Jesus said neither. He was drawing a line. He was making it known that disabilities were not directly tied to what a person or their lineage had done. Traditionally it was implied that either God or his right hand man would have cursed this man due to some sin either he or his family had committed. Jesus' teachings flew in the face of common teachings of his time and culture. Jesus was a rebel and counter cultural in his day, and it cost him his life. You couldn't be that diametrically opposed to religion and power in those days without getting snuffed out. Having said that, even Jesus said some stuff that would not be morally accepted today, but lets just leave that one alone. I also believe many attributes and claims were made of Jesus that he never made about himself. The same is being done with the Bible now. Christianity is making such drastic claims and placing such weight on the bible that it cannot hold up under the weight.

Much of these problems I blame on the early Roman church when attempting to make Christianity palatable to an empire. Had church leaders carried this type of a view of scripture and their faith, then they would have had answers for me, or they could've helped me seek them out. On further consideration, maybe I would have never had the questions to begin with because I would have never been taught that God quite literally has a higher kill count than Satan. Had the pastors, deacons, and mentors not had such a rigid view of Christianity then maybe they wouldn't have been inclined to call me a heretic. Do you know how hard it is to sit and hear a mentor call you a heretic? I quite literally had to leave the Christian faith to gain answers to the questions I had. When one begins to ask questions, it turns out that the world that Christianity claims to save me from, is more open and sympathetic than the church. The "World" tends to provide more sound answers than Christianity does. This isn't me speaking out in bitterness. This is me making an honest critique. This is me asking any Christian who may read this book to reconsider the damaging ways that Christianity does faith. Please reconsider and please change. It is the only way Christianity will survive, if it isn't too late already. If we could use the creation story to share with people how the very force, the very energy that created the universe also created you. This force literally breathed itself into you and is the very thing that sustains your life. That force, that energy still remains in every single person. We carry it on. We keep it alive. You were given that spark of life even while you were in your mother's womb. If this is how I came to be then that must mean that the homeless person, the homosexual, the Muslim, the Jew, literally everyone in existence was created the same way. Every person who ever existed carries the same value that I do. I believe that if Christianity had a similar approach to this, then Christianity would not have so many opponents. If all the Abrahamic religions all actually taught and believed this, then these religions could actually be used to bring the world together as one unified humanity. It would be much harder for nations to unify behind these religions, and as such would most likely not beat the war drums of whatever nations they serve.

One of the problems with Christianity though seems to be the pride taken in having enemies. It takes pride in people lashing out against the faith. It is essentially taken as a sign of the church "doing things right". It's kinda like a good aftershave, the stinging pain lets you know it's working. It believes it is being countercultural or standing against evil, but fails to see it is part of the problem. It is much like a person unaware of their harmful behavior while everyone around them is asking them to stop. The thought is that if the church did not have these naysayers, then it would be too palatable and too easy on the "sinner." You see so many Christian denominations splitting into yet another denomination normally because a group of people within that denomination consider their current teachings too easy and sugar coated. As such, Christianity needs haters the same way that some people thrive on drama. In their current forms they are mostly used to boast how one denomination is different and better than the other. Religion today is so often used to separate and divide rather than to unite. As such, the Abrahamic religions have probably been the most divisive, hateful, and bloodiest religions to ever exist. They have arguably done much more harm than good. A very good argument could be made that the earth would be a better place had they never existed. Both Christianity and the bible were never intended to carry the weight that is placed on them today, therefore when a person applies simple scrutiny, the same scrutiny that we apply to anything else, the bible and Christianity both in their current forms, simply collapse. Even though I sympathize with today's atheists and find myself agreeing with much of what they have to say, I believe many atheists are only atheistic against an Abrahamic type of god. If I had a choice between a god such as Yahweh, or to be an atheist, I would choose atheism all day long. I believe that since many have only been given a narrow window through which to view god, most find this view to be too narrow and unappealing. Since god has essentially been portrayed as a Zeus like figure, some do not consider the concept of a different type of power, a power much different and much more pure than just "god." To many the only other choice is to simply not believe in any theistic power at all. If a person is given a choice for all of their life, that they must either believe in what is given to them, or not believe at all, then we cannot blame them if they simply choose to not believe at all, without even considering the possibility of a much greater power being out there. In short, I believe the Abrahamic religions are once again their own greatest enemy and are almost solely responsible for the atheist movement today. This is a subject I wish to dig in to a little deeper later on. I want to be clear that I do not dislike atheists at all. I actually believe most atheist's beliefs to come from their hearts and their moral standards to supersede that of Christianity. If an atheist is kind to you, it is because that person is doing so from his or her heart. They are not trying to evangelize, gain brownie points, or further some ministry. They are kind because it's who they are, simple as that. It is kindness and love in its purest form. I find that the kindness and love coming out of an atheist exemplifies the pure divine consciousness inside of us all. If an atheist is to disagree with this then so be it. I have no problem with that. This is simply how it appears to me through my lenses.

CHAPTER 7:

BORDERS

WHEN THINKING OF BORDERS, WE often think of physical borders such as properties, cities, states, and nations. This is of course accurate, but far from complete. We can put up emotional walls or borders within ourselves. A nation's ideologies can be spread around the world and impact other nations. We can place spiritual or religious borders, excluding those of a different religion or belief system. Even these emotional and religious borders can range all the way from national borders to personal borders. These borders can also transcend nationality and can stretch far across the oceans and continents. Religious organizations and their doctrinal borders can stretch around the globe. If a nation, religion, or any group says that you must believe like us in order to be a part of us, then that group has just placed a border between itself and the rest of humanity. If you must believe, act, or look like me in order to be "in" then I have just isolated myself the same way that a nation's borders can isolate itself from everyone else. Personal trauma can cause a micro border to be placed around oneself that can get in the way of an otherwise close and intimate relationship. As we can see, borders range from all different sizes and types. Not all boundaries or borders are necessarily bad. If I have a very "needy" friend who wants me all to him or herself, then I need to place some boundaries to preserve my wellbeing. Some people will flat out suck the energy right out of you if you don't place some very clearly defined "borders". You don't want someone parking their car in the middle of the interstate or in the middle of your yard. There are parking areas and driveways that are clearly designated with "borders" around them that you can park your car in. So, we can see there are many uses for borders and some of those uses are good. When borders are drawn by institutions however, these borders can and have easily been used to leverage great evil and have cost many people their precious lives. If any group draws a line in the sand and calls itself exclusive, then this leads to a view of its patrons and members as being special and quite often superior. This is almost always a recipe for disaster, yet we see these types of groups and organizations all around us.

Often times emotional borders that we place between ourselves and loved ones come from some sort of pain or trauma that we experienced in life. I know that experiences I had in my past cause me to place relational and emotional walls between myself and my wife and children. By doing so this also causes me to perpetuate or pass on my own trauma to my loved ones. In other words, if I suffered from a feeling of being rejected and generally unwanted, I may put up a wall between myself and loved ones such as my children. This can then in return cause my children to feel rejected or unwanted. I can only hope that I realize this enough that the severity of rejection that my loved ones feel is simply not as severe as my past experiences. Hopefully I can also work on bringing down my walls to minimize the negative impact that I have on my loved ones. If I make enough progress, then hopefully I can help facilitate the healing of my loved ones and help them bring down their walls as well. If I intentionally work at this and my children and their children do the same, then hopefully we can work towards a world with a little less pain in it. In order for this to happen however, I must first start with myself. I first need to realize that I do have walls up. I need to realize, at least in part, why these walls were erected. I will also need to do some real work to be able to take these walls down. I will need to expose areas of my life that have been hidden for many years. I will need to give loved ones access to areas of my life that have not been touched by another person for many years. I will need to realize that I need to do this even with the fear of rejection being present. This is not a fun task, and any romantic notion of this process will quickly go away if one seriously takes on the task of healing.

Most of the time our motivation to change comes through pain and anxiety. Pain and anxiety are not just automatically bad. If seeing dirty dishes in the sink doesn't at least give me some anxiety, then I may never do dishes, or I may allow them to build up until my anxiety level builds high enough to force me to clean dishes. Where I get into trouble is when I ignore the anxiety for so long that it becomes a part of my life, a feeling that has found a home and no longer serves as a motivator but, now serves as a source of depression. Pain works the same way. Pain is not bad. Sometimes you need to invite pain in, and allow yourself to truly feel it. The pain that we avoid normally just continues knocking at the door.

Sometimes, in order for it to truly go away, you need to invite it in, have some tea with it, then let it go. Sometimes, when I allowed myself to feel pain, I wondered why I fought against it for so long. When I gave it space, it often showed me why I was hurting and enabled me to heal. I found I could often push through the pain like a wet napkin. Once faced, it often ended up being my friend. I did not invite it in to stay, but rather let it in, much like you do a friend, realizing they will leave when its time.

I began my journey of self-improvement several years ago when the pain of staying the same became greater than the pain of changing. The pain of living the way I was became so great that I was willing to move through the painful process of losing my religion, being rejected by loved ones and friends, and the pain of losing the false person that I had turned myself into. Realizing all the false identities and false attributes that you have sold yourself out to can be an extremely painful thing. All I knew is that the fire of the hell that I found myself in was unbearable and I needed to begin the process of getting out of it. For some of us, the pain that is required to get us to move is greater than for others. Some of this may be because of personality or how entrenched we are in our belief systems. For me, I was whole heartedly sold out on many different ideologies and beliefs. I believed that my conservative, nationalistic, religious, country upbringing (and all that it entailed) was the absolute and only right way to be. I could not wrap my brain around other thought processes, and thus, could not see the world through anyone else's perspective. My way of looking at things was undoubtedly right in my mind. My nationalistic and political views were founded and based upon my religious views. These undoubtedly had to be right as well because they were given to me in such a sure and matter of fact way. I couldn't see how a "liberal" could even be a true Christian, therefore anyone outside of conservative Americanism was essentially bidding for the downfall of America, which was essentially working against the will of God Himself. In this light it was so easy for people in this circle to call others outside of these borders the supposed antichrist, and indeed many were. I don't know how many political leaders and public figures were called the antichrist, but many were. I was so blinded to any other perspective that I couldn't even see the harm that was inflicted on me by this system. Damage inflicted even during my own child- hood. If what I had was so right, then how could the things done to me by this system be so wrong? Right? I was an easily influenced person, especially during my younger years. I mean who isn't right? I would say I was exceptionally "moldable" though. If you were older and even held a slightly significant role in family, church, or anything like that within our circle, then you could've had great influence on me. I still have the tendency to believe someone before I think they are a lying. I give people the benefit of the doubt most times, so think of how gullible I was as a child and young adult. I say all of that to bring out an understanding of the immense amount of falseness that was concealing the truth of who I was. I found myself living out of so many falsehoods that I had no clue who I truly was. I of course didn't know all of this when I began the journey, I just knew that I was willing to do just about anything in order to find the truth. I didn't know what all this journey would cause me to evaluate. I had no idea what it would ask me to lay down and what it would ask me to hold on to. All I knew was that my life wasn't working. What I believed wasn't working. What I was told would help me, and what was to be my saving grace fell way short of their promises. The pain became too much. My anxiety levels were so high that I physically hurt. I had to move. I honestly and truly hope that not many are as narrow minded and stubborn as I was. I hope that many will begin to move and question things long before the pain and anxiety become unbearable.

If there was a positive to all of this, it was that waiting to move until things were so bad for me, caused me to move quickly and plow ahead regardless of the opposition. I just knew that whatever I did, I just needed to keep moving. Stagnation is death. It wasn't all painful. I eventually became comfortable with change and looked at my journey as an adventure. I would never go back, and I am so glad that I began, but there are some parts that I hope I never have to do again. I say all of this to point out that all of those ideologies I had were all walls that I built between myself and reality. They all seemed to come together as one big fortress. They isolated myself in my own little world. It kept me away from so many people, even the ones I loved the most. I was surrounded by so many people, yet I remained lonely inside. Sometimes this is a defense mechanism, and sometimes these are constructed through world views that have been passed along to us. Either way, we all have these walls up in one form or another and we cannot demonize anyone else for guarding themselves differently than us. That is what it really comes down to. We tend to not understand the problems that we see in others, but we can come up with every reason in the world for our own problems and to keep our walls standing tall. We also can't be too hard on ourselves. It's a balancing act. We have to realize that either through pain or a series of hand me downs, we often built these walls before we were fully developed as a person, and to a large extent built them in order to survive. I know it isn't fair at all, but most of our walls were at least in part co-constructed with others. Even if others caused us to build them, only we can take them down. We can gain important knowledge, love, and compassion from others, others can hold your hand along the way, but we hold sole responsibility to bring down unhealthy barriers once we see them.

Even though changes are painful, for me they were still easier than living in my old place of indoctrinated coma. Don't get me wrong, I have not "arrived" anywhere and there are still layers that need to be peeled back, and there's still healing to be done, but I have begun and things have become easier. I have more happiness, and many of my old anxieties simply do not grip me anymore. I will say that the tearing down of my religious and nationalistic walls and borders were probably the most difficult ones in their own moments, however tearing down emotional walls and those pertaining to relationships have been the most ongoing and fatiguing ones. Emotional and relational walls are probably my most numerable and most well-built walls. This was true for me, however I am sure others have varied experiences. There are areas that are still walled off, and the areas that I have opened have been very difficult and time consuming. It takes so much conscious and continued effort. Once you see the truth of religion and nationalism, they almost crumble on their own (more on that later), but not emotional ones. Don't get me wrong, religious and nationalistic tendencies take intentionality and effort as well, and it is not a comfortable place to be. I am sure that for some this experience could be different. There is no "one size fits all" experience in this. Looking at emotional and relational walls and realizing they need to come down has been harder for me overall. The very act of opening yourself up to other people invariably opens yourself up to more pain. If you truly open up to a spouse or partner, will they still love you? Will they think you are weak when they see your soft side? Will they think you are a monster if they see your dark side? If you open yourself up to truly loving and cherishing your children, what will happen if you tragically lose one? What if you truly allow yourself to love your partner, what happens if they leave you or choose someone else? These are very real questions, but they are rooted in fear. Fear cannot be something that inhibits your journey. None of them can be answered until you live it out. All I know is that being a shell of a human and not feeling true emotions is way worse than opening up and feeling pain. Sometimes if you have been numb for so long, the feeling of pain can be refreshing, because you finally just feel something. I remember moments like this. I had felt little to nothing for so long that it actually felt good to hurt. Being numb and ignoring or avoiding emotion is easier in a short term basis, but in the long run it becomes torture. Sometimes the feeling of pain means you are making progress. Don't avoid it. The famous saying of "having loved and lost is better than never having loved at all" comes to mind. Most of the time, if you have good people around you and you do not reciprocate back to them the love that they need, you will probably lose them anyway, so do not be afraid to love. You stand a much greater chance of heartache if you do not allow yourself to love than if you just give it all you've got. Unfortunately, this area in my life is still the area that I struggle with the most. Trust me, I'm not there yet either. In my opinion, I have more walls up in my relationships than anywhere else. I am trying to move forward and improve in this area, but for me it is very hard, and it takes a bunch of work. Even though relationships come easy to some people, I would say that emotional and relational walls would probably be the toughest ones to bring down. I have never heard of a person reaching their final end in this existence and expressing the regret of loving too much. I have also never heard of a grieving person mourning the loss of a loved one, wishing they had loved their loved one less in order to ease the pain of the loss. I have however heard many people wishing they would have better cherished the time they did have with their loved lost ones. In the areas of love and relationship we find the most deep and fulfilling things we can ever experience, and yet they tend to be the hardest ones to truly open up to. You can take one's nation, home, and career away from someone, but if you leave them surrounded by loved ones, they will normally survive just fine. Losing a loved one on the contrary, will often make a person not care about physical things and only wish to have a bit more time with the ones they love. If the fear of loss keeps you from loving, then we must realize that the time will come when we truly will lose everyone. The thing of it is that we will undoubtedly lose every one that is near and dear to us. At some point and time everyone will leave for college, get married, move to a new country, die (in so many different ways), etc. We never get to choose how we lose someone, so we had might as well love as hard as we can while we can. In the end it will probably be the only thing that really matters. In the end the pain of not loving the people around you will probably far outweigh the pain of losing the people around you.

So, what about actual physical borders? I honestly don't know where I stand on this subject. I see benefits and problems from both having borders, and from not having borders. We tend to draw borders from very large areas all the way down to the very small. On the large scale we separate continents. Within those continents we place nations, then something on the order of states or territories. Within these states we have more localized ones such as counties, then cities, towns municipalities and all the way down to personal property lines, such as farms, and down to city lots. It is all rather orderly in a way, and it does allow for more localized governments to cater to a more localized culture. To clarify, the North American culture is vastly different than an Asian or African culture. It would be very difficult for one governing body to meet the needs of all the different cultures and people groups across the globe. I think we see this from examples such as the former Soviet Union or the Roman Empire attempting to govern too vast of a region. I know there are fine details to this, but ultimately the needs of different countries and cultures became too polarized to all fit under one governing body. We see this going on today where the Uyghurs, Kazakhs, Kyrgyz, and various other Turkic Muslims in Xinjiang, China are being targeted with forced abortions, sterilization, rape, forced labor and many other things by the Chinese government. The people of Xinjiang at large do not want Chinese government, and the Chinese government is attempting a forced integration into the Chinese culture. This government and culture flies in the face of what the people of Xinjiang want and need. This is a great example of what a localized and dogmatic government does when it attempts to reach too far and govern too many different people groups. In order for this to work out in any humane way at this point, would be for China to release Xinjiang from the Chinese borders and allow the district to govern itself as their own sovereign culture, or for China to allow a culture to thrive in their own unique way inside of its borders. The problem with the latter is that it would require a nation to completely rework how it operates, which would be good, but unlikely. Secondly, national borders were often drawn without consideration of dividing cultures. This often leads to a line being drawn right through a culture, splitting it in two. Nations such as China would need to allow for the free movement of people through its border in order to allow similar cultures, that have been split by borders, to intermingle.

This kind of exemplifies the problem we have with national borders as well. In order for borders to work in the best interest of humanity then governments must truly place the wellbeing of people first. Governments must first wish to see all people flourish, even if it means to let them go. National interests must not be so self-centered that it overlooks the intricate needs of the people it is attempting to govern. If it comes down to a certain government style suiting one group and not another, then at the least there needs to be room for different governing styles to be implemented. The other example in current affairs is Russia's attempt at annexing the Ukraine. This is an ongoing conflict as I write this, with the "invasion" of Ukraine just being undertaken. Russia sees the Ukraine as being a part of itself, and yet Ukraine wishes largely to be an independent nation. The West of course is not blameless in this. The West has been meddling in this situation for decades now. The economy and "puppet" government we worked to install is actually part of the problem. Of course I do not agree with Russia, however I think Russia and Putin are not to take all the blame. I quite honestly think Russia has been demonized by the West for so long and Putin is simply tired of our shit. I'm sure Russia demonized the West as well. We should all be tired of shit coming from both the "Eastern" and "Western" powers. What Russia is doing in Ukraine is only a mirror reflection of what United States and Western powers did in Iraq not even twenty years ago. Sure some details are different, however from the Russian view of things, they are just as justified right now as we were then, or any war the United States has fought since WW II for that matter. This conflict and ruffling of feathers by world powers is exactly what nations do, and they will never stop under their current configuration. This is nations doing what nations do. Always have. Sure, it would serve the Russian interest to annex Ukraine, however this would lead to the death of thousands and thousands of people through an ongoing power struggle that would probably last for years. However, the "West" was hard at it to take the vast resources of Ukraine for itself. The "West" was doing covertly through economic games, what Russia is doing outrightly for all to see. The Ukrainian sovereignty was never going to last with our meddling in it, and what's worse, we knew it. In my opinion, the Western powers do not care about Ukrainian sovereignty anymore than Russia does. That is partially why we would not give Ukraine admission into NATO. We knew Russia would push back the same way we did against Soviet influence in Korea, Vietnam, and Cuba. If the "West" truly cared for Ukraine, we would have helped them set up a government that was not so polarized, that would not have been so catered to one side or the other. But we didn't, and we knew that bringing them into NATO would lead to eventual war with Russia, leading to another World War, if it hasn't already. This is quite literally a mirror reflection of what the "West" has been doing for decades. Once again, I do not condone or agree in any way the actions of Russia right now. Russia is every bit as corrupt as the "West". I am merely asking "what did we expect?" Looking back on the history of this situation we should have (and did) seen this coming miles away. Now we want to sit and act shocked at Russia's actions. It was expected. I am by no means taking Russia's side on this. I do not see it as a dualistic fight of goof vs evil either. What Russia is doing is horrible and should be heavily condemned, but for us to only place blame on Russia and act as though they were unprovoked is a show of pure ignorance. NATO and the West acting like big brats, sat and poked the bear with a sharp stick and wondered why it bit back. This is what the world's powers have been doing for thousands of years. It is nothing new. We should all be sick and tired of it. If we do not change this, we will just be perpetuating this vicious cycle. It will not end on its own. The "West" is already conniving how it will undermine a new "Eastern" Ukrainian government. They are essentially trying to figure out how to keep Ukraine under perpetual torment, a hell of sorts. Maybe we need to ask who the real Satan is in this world, and who the creators of hell really are. God isn't coming back to stop it either, and for some he is creating it "all for His glory, Hallelujah and amen." Some people in America are actually saying that god is using Putin to do His/God's work by destroying evil powers and such. People are saying this is the work of God! Can you believe this? This goes to show how evil they think god is. Some of it, maybe most of it, is political, saying that Trump was striking up relations with Russia and now Putin is essentially taking over where Trump left off. This of course is to say, once again, that God is ok with the death and suffering of innocent people in order to get His way. Their political views have become so massive that it blocks any other form of rational. The left is just as evil by solely demonizing Russia and Putin. The ignorance is astounding. We need to stop suffering under this as a necessary evil of sorts, and actually do something about it. In order for nations to coexist and for national borders to continue to work, then the governments must truly seek what is best for the people of the world, not for the wellbeing of the nation. The attempted subjugation of the people by China, Russia, The UK, USA, and all major powers and factions clearly exemplifies the fact that the world and its governments simply are not there yet. Governments are acting in a very narcissistic way. Why would China, Russia or any other nation including the United States be willing to oppress and kill so many people just to force them to live inside their borders, or to hoard resources for themselves. It makes absolutely no sense. This however is the way governments have operated since the dawn of so called civilization. If we do not want a repeat of the twentieth century then society needs to reevaluate government and how it should operate. Under its current configuration, we will always have war, genocide, and nations living in prosperity and luxury while others struggle to survive. The thing of it is that the situations in Russia and China are nothing new. Almost every continent and dominant nation that exists today is guilty of this very thing. America did this during its establishment through the wholesale slaughter of indigenous tribes. We did this even later after Mexico had been an established nation. We wanted Texas so we stole it fair and square. Australia did this to its Aboriginal people. The list goes on and on. The thing of it is that it just seems that nations seem to find themselves at these horrible places at different times. We're all guilty of it. The thing with Russia and China is that they find themselves in an era where news travels quickly and the gory mess of it all can be streamed in color into the homes of everyone across the globe. We have a media that can twist the "truth" into anything they want. When something like this is seen by people who do not realize the horrors of war, it comes as a shock. This causes the population in general to become outraged at the dominant nation almost regardless of the situation. On a good note, this brings out people's humanity. Humanity in its pure form always supersedes nationalism. We only need to realize that when our nation does the same thing, it appears just as gruesome to everyone else, no matter how justified we feel in our actions.

I do believe that borders could be used to benefit the whole world if they are used in the right way. They shouldn't be used to divide one people group from another in some superior or exclusive way. They should not be used to claim rights to prosperity as if someone inside a nation's borders has some special rights to life. They could however be used to recognize different cultures and their sovereignty, value, and strength. Travel, commerce, and overall economic wellbeing should not be restricted by these lines. The goods and prosperity of one region should be equally available to all people. If you wish to live as a certain culture does, you should be free to go there and do so. If business and trading could be done in areas of the globe where it makes the most sense rather than trying to keep them exclusively for one nation, then wealth and prosperity could be shared globally. I don't see this as a way of bringing down the prosperous, but rather making prosperity available to everyone. I think there are enough resources available for everyone. I don't think the world is lacking in any way when it comes to resources. We are lacking in our willingness to share in a charitable way. I am not attempting to bring about global socialism either. Socialism is a current system used that has also failed many times. Think outside the box of current systems and continue with the theme of discovering something new and possibly completely different from anything attempted before. A community sharing its talents, resources, and knowledge doesn't deserve to be placed inside a current economic or political system. I am also not a proponent of huge government entities managing or overseeing all of this. Government in its simplest form is there to provide an environment that is healthy for people to flourish. Government may be able to subsidize programs to a degree, but normally become very inefficient at running programs outright. One example is the United States space program. It became so inefficient that it actually regressed in its development and essentially shut down large parts of its program. The good thing to this is that it opened up a vacuum that private enterprise capitalized on to fill the gap. Private rocket companies are springing up everywhere and they are doing it better than the government ever would have. They are reusing rockets and bringing down the cost of space flight exponentially. They are operating with a flexibility and ingenuity that government simply cannot do. The reuse of rockets is something that only an outside perspective of the industry came up with. The privatization of space flight has also opened up the ability for one of these private companies to supply internet coverage to the half of the world's population that previously had none. The privatization of an industry that was previously a government monopoly not only opened up new opportunities in space, but enabled a private company to also help out the global community. The government being the monopoly on space flight had essentially closed itself off from innovation. The repeated use of the same old companies to produce its products also in part led to the grossly overpriced cost of any of its programs. Private companies are developing and building completely new rocket systems for less than what NASA can produce using recycled systems. The lack of competition had led to the lack of ingenuity and a disregard to cost savings. This isn't a knock on NASA itself. If

NASA were not so influenced by government and politics, it would probably be just fine. The government with NASA had pursued the idea of re-landing a human on the moon, but quickly found itself so mismanaged and over budget that it has essentially suspended the endeavor indefinitely. This is no attempt at degrading the truly great achievements of the astronauts and all who participated in space travel. The brilliance and courage required to accomplish what they did is astounding. We also need to remember that the government's space industry was foundationally flawed from its origins. The United States' space industry was conceived during the cold war in competition with another nation. It was hastily thrown together and somewhat carelessly managed in order to assert dominance over the former Soviet Union. It was politically motivated. In doing so, it could be argued that it was less about science and the advancement of the human race, and more about asserting dominance over the world. This in a humorous way is much akin to one dog humping another dog just to show who is boss of the back yard, when they could both equally enjoy the space together. Why couldn't nations such as the USA and Soviet Union not come together and work together to reach the moon. Their accomplishments would have probably been greater and manned space exploration probably would not have stagnated through elimination of the competition.

If competition amongst nations would cease, then the people of each nation could focus on developing their strengths and sharing it with the world. Rather than a nation needing to thrive in all industries, it could focus on thriving in its strongest areas and then sharing that with the world. Anything that one nation lacks can be supplied by another. I know that to some degree this is done today, but it has a political and greedy undertone to it all, and it is not done to the extent that is possible. This would also eliminate the forceful acquisition of other nations such as Russia's attempt at annexing the Ukraine. If everyone interacted freely and things were not done for power and selfish gain, there would be absolutely no need to do such things. This of course would take the reconsideration and restructuring of the most prominent governments. Governments would need to completely redefine themselves and their purpose in society. Private industries would also need to rethink some things. The thinking and mentality of it all would need to change. Even in private industry, advancement in a field is normally closely guarded in an attempt to exclusively hang on to that achievement for personal gain. I am however, unwilling to hear that the proper changes could not be made or that this is an unrealistic way of looking at things. I don't think the world has ever tried to exist this way. I know we couldn't just step into it flawlessly and I don't know when the right time would be to do it. I don't even know the proper way to do all of this. Maybe there is no singular point that would ever be right. Maybe it needs to be an evolutionary change. Something that society simply moves into over time, unhindered by governments and politics that thrive by keeping things the same. I just have the belief that in order for humanity to prosper and live together we need to at least start moving in a different direction. Are we always going to live this way? I know some people tend to think this is just how it is. Some believe things will be this way and possibly get worse until the "Lord comes back". This type of thinking is counter progressive and only holds society back. This type of thinking is quite literally the enemy to change and the advancement of society. This is one of the reasons why I say that nationalism and religion are the two main hinderances to society and mankind. According to Christianity, this is just part of a fallen world and it only destined to get worse, so why even try? The pursuit of world peace is treated as if one is literally acting against the will of God. Christianity is a defeated mindset that always looks through a victim mentality. The cause is always defeated before it is even begun, so most good change is never even attempted.

Think about it. Why does China need Xinjiang in order to benefit from it? Why does Russia need to own Ukraine in order to share resources and culture? The only reason is if there is a view of exclusivity. They and most nations still believe that in order to benefit from something they need to possess it. When they do possess it, their intention is to exclusively own those people and resources, and if there is enough left over to be given out to others, it will be peddled out in such a way that it still brings exclusive benefit to the nation that possesses it. The crazy part of it is that these nations are also claiming possession of the people of the land they own. People are still owned by a nation the same way that a nation owns the mineral rights within its borders. There is something very unsettling about this. This is all about power and the betterment of one nation at the expense of another. There is something so wrong with the fact that a few people in leadership positions can be so convinced and set on an idea that they are willing to sacrifice innumerable lives on the altar of nationalism. This however is at least in part a societal problem. Most of these ideas and leaders are merely a product of society. Society itself needs to change before the change will reach government. I believe society has changed and is in the middle of making a huge shift, but the current governmental system is trying to stay the same. It is almost a battle between humanity and the systems we created. I believe that the way to continue this change in society is to bring it into your own life, and not let current systems snuff it out. If one person at a time will commit to changing themselves, then eventually it will become the new normal. We can only change ourselves. Rather than focusing on eating the whole watermelon in one huge bite, we need to focus on small bites. If we try to bring about change by demanding it ultimately in one massive swoop, then the change will ultimately always be untimely and impossible. Society will never be ready for change if it is required to make the changes all at once and in one large leap. Maybe instead of brainstorming in an attempt at dream up a new system, we could all implement the change we want to see into our own lives. As enough people do this, the change would take care of itself automatically without the intentional implementation of a global system. Envision a world, if reincarnation were real, that you would want to come back to. Think about this as if you may randomly come back as human or animal in the future. Would you want to come back to this same thing? Do you want your grandchildren to live in the current reality of this world? Don't think that your God will come back before then. God has been expected to return for two thousand years and it still hasn't happened. Don't use your religion as an excuse to stay the same. Don't use your ideas of reality to punish everyone else. Even if you believe in a God coming back soon, still push for change just in case you are wrong. We always teach our children that something is only impossible if they don't try. Even if you think your goal is impossible, you still need to envision a life the way that it should be and try to get as close to that as possible.

CHAPTER 8:

MY EXPERIENCE

PURELY FOR THE SAKE OF context and to help shed light on where all of this is coming from, I will give a brief description of my past. Like everything in this book, this is not an in depth dive, but rather a skimming over for the sake of context. I am also not writing anything below to be overly critical. I was born into an Amish family in rural America. My family did leave the Amish religion with a period of entering a Mennonite type of sect during my younger years. I was raised on farms into my teenage years. In fact, my parents owned a farm for a short portion of my childhood. I have some of the best memories a kid could have of roaming free. We had plenty woods, streams, and fields to roam and explore. We spent most of our days outside. I grew up hunting and fishing and just generally enjoying the great outdoors. Myself and my siblings began helping on farms at a young age. I remember driving tractors before I could properly reach the pedals and I was slinging hay bales before my teenage years. Between eighth and ninth grade we moved from rural Pennsylvania to a city in Florida. The change of space, culture, and the loss of friends was shocking to me. I very quickly got into drugs and alcohol. I got my first real job on a construction crew when I was fourteen. I was the first in my family to continue school through high school. I maintained my construction job after school hours and worked full time during the summer months. This is not to be used to say my family is uneducated or simple in any way. Most of my family are successful entrepreneurs, owning their own businesses and blazing their own trails. During high school, 9/11 happened. Being the patriotic young man that I was, I enlisted in the military. I went to basic training in 2003 and deployed later that same year. I came back from that deployment not even old enough to drink yet. Religiously I had given up on Christianity during my teenage and military years due to several reasons. I had a lot of bitterness against God for the loss or injury of a couple friends. These were all very good men. I saw the horror of war and thought God to be the creator of it all. This just didn't make any sense to me with my understanding of an all powerful God who was responsible for all things that happen. Post military, I went through a painful separation from my fiancé, all the while struggling through my military separation and some experiences I had there. I was a young man just trying to make sense of it all, and nothing did make sense. My ex-fiancé and I had been together a long time, including through my military service and the breakup was very difficult. In my early twenties I limped back home to my family who were mostly living in Florida at the time. I was an extremely broken young man on so many different levels, and from so many different things. There my family had taken up Christianity with a new vigor, which very quickly gripped me as well. I became a very devout and religious

Christian. Christianity is the bandage that held me together for many years as I suffered through some very painful times. Without going into too much detail, Christianity did extend a saving hand to me and did help me survive these painful years. It did give a sense of comfort and belonging that I desperately needed. It also dangled healing and hope in front of me like dangling a carrot in front of a horse and never letting it reach it. In that way Christianity held me together, by giving me hope and a sense of community, but keeping things just out of reach. It did fail to truly heal me and seemed to serve more like a bandage that held my severed limbs together while unseen infections festered underneath. I do believe that even though Christianity did save me in a way, there would have been more wholesome and life giving options out there. Christianity could have also been more helpful had Christianity developed in a healthier way. Getting back to the story, I continued with my conservative religious and political views for many more years. I did find another young lady a couple years later. We were married after a short dating period. Needless to say, I was still way under equipped and way too broken to enter into a marriage. Thankfully the both of us are fighters and we generally do love each other, so we have held on to each other to this day. We have two beautiful children as well. Thankfully we both were in need of change, and we were both open minded enough to reconsider our belief systems. I will not speak for my wife and talk about her journey, however she has been open and strong enough to stick with me through mine. Today I do not claim to be either on the "right" or the "left" when it comes to politics or religion. I do not hold to many Christian beliefs. I do not want to paint myself into a corner by labeling myself. I do however believe in divinity, and that all humans and all known things somehow contain and exemplify a divine power or energy. Some people and things may have strayed down a path where we may not be manifesting things in the beautiful way that we could be. Maybe we as a species are coming from a place of darkness and we all as a collective being are on a journey towards light. I do not believe in a physical "god" but I do believe in a higher power, whatever that may look like. I actually think that the traditional view of what the word "god" means has ruined the view many people have of divinity. I don't think divinity looks anything like "god", but our traditional language simply does not have many other words to describe it.

Considering the background given above, you can use that to imagine the lenses I viewed the world through for the better part of my life. I had deep conservative nationalistic and religious views. When I say that I was a Christian, I mean that I took it very seriously and quite literally believed my life depended on it. I wasn't just a "pew sitter". When I say that I was nationalistic, I mean that I believed the United States and the people in it was the one nation that mattered the most. The USA was in my view the final home of freedom in the world, and we were essentially God's last stronghold in this world. In my view at the time, if the USA failed then there would be no good place left and it was our duty to enforce freedom across the globe. I did not just believe these things. I was an active participant in it. You can imagine then how much pain and anxiety it caused me to even consider taking these religious and nationalistic views into question.

My nationalism and my political views were also so intertwined with my religion that you almost couldn't tell them apart. You can imagine very easily how you can quickly put walls up and view people outside of both your nation and religion as being something "other" and something to guard against. Because my religious beliefs were so intertwined and similar to my political and nationalistic views, when I questioned one it immediately led to questioning the other. The thing that led to all this questioning wasn't because I wanted to question it. It came from a place of realizing that my faith simply wasn't working for me. My life was in such shambles for so long that I simply could not ignore it. Couple that together with a couple of events that felt like a misleading by the church, and it kind of kept rolling from there. I decided to dig into church history to find answers for myself. I wanted to know where our beliefs came from. I did not know that questioning a place of eternal torment could even be done. I literally had no clue that a large portion of Christianity did not necessarily adhere to this. I also had no clue where our canon of scripture came from either. I had no idea that there was a huge range of beliefs as to what the canon was or should be. I had no clue as to how they decided which books to keep. I didn't even know there were many other books that were destroyed and that many of the current books are still disputed. When it came to "The Trinity" I had no clue that the views of this were heavily disputed since the founding of Christianity. I thought there was essentially one way to look at the Trinity and there were no real competing views. Digging into all of these things I also learned about the early church fathers. Prior to this I considered people like Martin Luther, John Calvin, John Wesley, and John Wycliffe as being our church fathers. I had no clue about the early church patriarchs such as Irenaeus, Augustine, Ignatius, Polycarp, Justin Martyr, and the list goes on. What I discovered is that church history was much deeper and much more vast than I had ever imagined. I also felt betrayed by the church because I knew that along the way, there were people who intentionally hid this information. I think this was done progressively by people long ago, and also by people, pastors, and gatekeepers today who simply did not want to divulge this information. After the protestant reformation, the Western Christian church lost its history, traditions, and sense of identity. We now have pastors who can go spew almost anything they want across a pulpit without truly knowing where their beliefs come from. Many people that are very religious and dogmatic in their beliefs are only aware of events happening in the last several hundred years. Some will demonize early church patriarchs and the early church in general, but do not realize many of their views of their faith such as the Trinity, bodily resurrection, etc… were hammered out by these same people.

What I discovered during my search were things that I thought would help ground me in Christianity at its truest form. I read early church fathers that talked about these deep things that were viewed very differently back then. I looked into lost gospels such as the gospel of Mary. They had great things to say and read from things that most people have never heard about. Why is this? I found out that during many of the councils that were held to hammer out the accepted texts, many early scriptures were deemed heresy and sometimes burned. This could be done by people who held the most power at the council. This power could come from relations with a government official, or by starting the council purposely before the believers of an opposing view even had the chance to show up. In those days the councils were held to set doctrine and establish scripture. The church leaders from across Europe, the Middle East, and Africa would have to attend. Many of these big councils were held through the fourth and fifth centuries. Travel took a long time. Sometimes when there were opposing views on how to view certain things such as the Trinity, an influential person would literally begin the council early knowing full well that a church leader with an opposing view was still on their journey to the council. This eliminated that opposition. Sometimes by the time a leader showed up to the council, they and their teachings or writings were already deemed heretical. They could be excommunicated and often exiled without even being present when the decision was made. Many female apostles and teachers and their writings were deemed heretical just because of their gender. The church forgets that according to biblical writing, a female was the first to share the gospel to the cowering male disciples. This is a long winded way of saying that many of our beliefs and doctrine were derived in similar fashion. The doctrines that became dominant became so not necessarily because they were the most popular and were voted on unanimously. Rather, many became dominant through political prowess or simply strong arming its way to the top. If a leader was deemed a heretic, then those following him would need to change their doctrine, at least in show, in order to not become heretics themselves. They needed to burn the writings of the ones deemed a heretic, so that they would not be burned as well. The councils were normally won through power and violence. Normally these councils were supposed to unite the church, but often times just led to more problems and disunity. Making a claim that this was an early church problem that no longer exists is, in my opinion a false claim. We have over forty thousand different denominations of Christianity, most of whom fall under Protestantism. Even Protestantism, which began under harsh persecution, burned its first heretic at the stake in order to eliminate a competing denomination. John Calvin, one of the protestant reformers was one person directly responsible for the burning to death of Michael Servetus on October 27, 1553, setting him ablaze on top of a pile of his own books. Some of these deadly disputes could partially be because of how someone referred to Jesus and the extent of his divinity, or what role the "Holy Spirit" played in the Trinity. Once again, most of these problems still have not been solved as most Christians cannot adequately explain the Trinity or how they all relate to each other. Many Christians can't even agree on whether other Christians in another denomination will even go to heaven or not. The Amish fully believe in the Trinity, but say that you cannot know for sure whether you are saved or not. They believe in a blessed hope that they will go to heaven. To them, you could be damned to hell for saying that you know you're not going there. Some outside the Amish religion would say that most Amish will not go to heaven since they do not profess to have an assurance of salvation, therefore they do not fully depend on the "Lord Jesus" as their savior. Using this logic and going down the rabbit hole, some would conclude that the Amish are not true Christians and therefore destined for hell. The Amish would claim that most Christians outside of the Amish would not be going to heaven because most Christians believe in faith alone to reach paradise, but do not have the proper actions or "works" to get there. The Amish still rely heavily on personal actions to get to heaven. Both sides of the argument are using scripture and very valid ones at that. Both sides claim to have the "Truth" with a capital "T" and both sides will not budge in their thinking. We have over forty thousand different variations of this silliness that proves that Christianity itself cannot even decide on what Christianity itself even is. This has been a dispute from the days of Paul and the actual disciples of Jesus. People directly following the man and people with "direct revelation" from him couldn't even decide what was right. How can you follow something that doesn't even know what it is?

If Protestantism had not attempted to forget its past or hide it from its lowly sheep, then maybe this all would not have been so shocking to me. Maybe this would not have been so overwhelming to me and would not have caused an "unraveling of the rug" so to speak. Oftentimes the withholding of the information in an attempt to "shepherd the flock" does the very thing they are attempting to eliminate. For most curious people, when they go in search of truth and find out that information was withheld, for whatever reason, will in itself cause the unraveling to begin. Even if the withholding of information happened hundreds of years ago, the fact remains that the spreading of misinformation is foundational to that particular belief system. For a system that portrays itself as the preserver of the word of God and its purity, it causes a huge black mark for people who have placed their trust in it. Even the early church fathers had some shocking things to say about the power and "infallibility" of its leaders. Ignatius in his letter to the Smyrnaeans wrote "You must follow the lead of the Bishop, as Jesus Christ followed that of the Father; follow the presbyter as you would the Apostles; reverence the deacons as you would God's commandment… Wherever the bishop appears, there let the people be, even as wheresoever Christ Jesus is…" This in any Christian account should be seen as giving too much power to leadership, bordering on heresy. Should we say it is "idolatrous?" Protestantism, even though it separated from the church did not so much make a clean break, but rather rearranged the furniture, gave some new names to it and called it a different house. They still do the same with preachers, teachers, deacons, etc… Also, Protestantism still adheres to the doctrines that were hammered out in the councils that these guys ran. The doctrine of the Trinity, the canon of scripture, and so many other doctrines that protestants use today are the same ones that found their origins during these times, hundreds of years after the days of Christ. Protestantism does not like to teach this history because to do so would be claiming common ancestry with the catholic church, and well, they're not really considered true Christians either. They like to teach these doctrines and read these scriptures without really telling you where they came from. Protestantism finds its roots in the Eastern Orthodox and Roman Catholic church, but tries to write them off like a disgruntled sibling attempting to disown another sibling. This doesn't work though, because in reality Protestantism is like a child attempting to disown its parents. You can deny it all you want, but they will always be your parents, and their past will always be your past as well. The DNA of the early church courses through Protestantism whether they like it or not. All the divisions, hatred, bigotry, narcissism, sexism, heresy, and death associated with the early church is likewise associated with Protestantism. In fact, Protestantism sort of carried some of these horrible things on. Like a relay racer passing the baton on to the next runner, Protestantism took the baton of bigotry, sexism, narcissism, hatred, and death and continued running with it. The same sins that Protestantism lays on the early church were committed by the Protestants as well.

Since my religion was so closely tied with my nationalism, I found my unraveling of nationalism to go much the same way. Digging into the true history of the United States led to much of the same dirt that I found under the rug of Christianity. This was also a journey of believing that The United States was kind of the pure form of nations the way Christianity was the pure form of religion. I had been taught a glossed over version of our history. I knew we had a black eye or two along the way, but overall was taught we had the best of intentions, and we ultimately only did things for the betterment of humanity. Once again, this untrue teaching of our history led to great distrust once I started learning the real truth to it all. It caused me to question everything about our nation. When something is placed on a pedestal in front of someone, as something to be revered and to hold in high esteem in such a large way, people tend to be much more critical of such a thing when the dirty truth comes out. The greater and more extraordinary the claims, the greater the criticism when the truth comes out. The crazy thing is, the less something props itself up as being this great thing, the greater it actually becomes. If something is just claimed to be no better or exceptional as everything around it, then the scrutiny will not be as great when the dirt inevitably reaches the surface. If the dirt and flaws of a system are taught and used as a reminder of the way even one's nation can use power for harm, then a much more constructive form of patriotism can arise. Maybe patriotism leaves a bad taste in some people's mouths because of how it has been used in place of nationalism. I would then say that one could hold all of humanity in higher regard. If you realize that your very own nation messed up in some very grotesque ways, then you would be more apt to realize that you are not exceptional just because you live in that nation. You will also be less likely to exploit peoples or lands in order to prosper your own. You will be less likely to promote war in a far off land when you realize that if you judged your own nation in the same manner, your nation would be just as deserving of being ravaged by war as any other nation. The dirty secrets should no longer be out there to discover on your own, but should rather be taught in public schools and in a constructive way.

CHAPTER 9:

SOCIETAL STRUCTURES

"The history of progress is written in the blood of
men and women who have dared to espouse an
unpopular cause, as, for instance, the black man's
right to his body, or a woman's right to her soul."

~Emma Goldman~

I KNOW THAT IN THIS book I keep coming back to religion and
nationalism over and over again, but religion and nationalism have
been so predominant in culture for most of human existence. So
many social structures, nations, perceptions, wars, lifestyles, and
borders have been built through religious and nationalistic pre-
suppositions. Most of our perceived world has been created by it.
Most of our systems have been created to prop up or support either
a nation or a religion, but normally both. Even areligious people
view their world through more religious constructs than they would

ever imagine. Religions of all sorts have been so tied together with national views that you often can't tell the two apart. Our very societies have been built on religion and nationalism, and to have a world view apart from those things is almost foreign to anyone, myself included. In life we believe that who we are depends so much on the social systems that we adhere to. We gain our identities through them. Our systemic social constructs are largely based on having THE truth and all the right answers. Nothing has brought me more healing and relieved me of more anxiety than the realization that I do not need to have all the answers. I am quite content that way actually. I don't claim to adhere to any religious or nationalistic views (yet I am sure I do without knowing it). I believe we have been conditioned to believe that our wellbeing depends so much on knowing the real truth, on having the right information, that we close ourselves off from anything that challenges our presupposed truths. By gaining our identity and wellbeing from our prescribed politics, nationalism, and religion it makes it almost impossible to live out of who we truly are. We live through these other ideas, systems, and manmade constructs. These constructs determine how we should act, what should offend us, how we should speak, treat others, and they even give us a prepackaged religion. They tell us what is morally acceptable, what our family structures should look like, what economies to support, and the list goes on. This has been the general formula for various societies for thousands of years. All of these things are given to us at a very young age, and we begin to live through them so quickly that many of us never got to know our true selves. Don't be surprised if you get back lash from people around you as you go down the path of self-discovery, because many of your loved ones have never met the real you either. Just like anyone, your friends and family would rather hang on to the old you rather than watch you change into something new. We tend to gravitate towards what is comfortable, which tends to be what we have known in the past. Don't forget that self-discovery is what this is all about. Most of the time we can only truly discover ourselves by peeling away the layers of beliefs that entities other than ourselves have placed on us.

The biggest hurdle with religion and nationalistic beliefs is just being willing to question them. I think that one of the things that makes it so hard to begin questioning Christianity is that you are literally warned against rationally questioning anything or pursuing greater knowledge or understanding prepackaged doctrines. Most of these doctrines were contrived many hundreds, if not thousands of years ago by some powerful men living in another space and time. You are essentially taught blind faith is the way to go on this. We were taught that having too many questions can lead you astray. Looking at this reasoning from the outside, it is very obvious that this system was developed to keep you from the truth. These national and religious systems are only unquestionable if they are trying to hold you prisoner and to suppress your own free thought. The church could only teach and sell indulgences to get family members out of purgatory by keeping the public masses in the dark. The same is true with tithing today. Any system built on the idea that you cannot question it is a weak system. The only reason why you would not be allowed to question a system, is because the questions will lead you towards the truth and away from that very system. Any system that claims you may not question it, must be questioned extensively just because of that premise alone. Christianity would say that it is open to questioning and scrutiny. It turns out this is only true if you stay within certain parameters. Once you go outside the prescribed documentation and acceptable questions, you are considered heretical and an in enmity with god. When it comes to Christianity, this system of non-questioning was developed in large during the powerful years of the Roman Catholic Church to keep the peasants in the dark. They were withholding information and even books to keep knowledge away from the common folk. Bibles were only written in Latin so that even if peasants would acquire one, they could not read them. This was only done because the powers of the time knew that if common people would gain knowledge, their lies would be exposed, and their reign of power would be over. In fact, there have been modern teachers who intentionally withhold information such as opposing thoughts from their congregants to "protect their flock". This very system has not fully been shed in Christianity and is also widely used by many nations to keep its citizens loyal to the state.

One of the ways that nations keep you going about your life unquestioningly is by attempting to gloss over the darker parts of its history. Most nations require a sense of exceptionalism to keep the loyalty of its citizens. If a nation can teach a history class to its students during their younger years, it can have major control over this in an attempt to gain loyal followers from its young people. The young people after all are the ones who will need to fight and die for the old powerful people's decisions. It will hit on some of the subjects briefly but won't dive in too deep, giving the appearance of a true history class. It will also spin the narrative to be viewed in the favor of the nation. I cannot remember who said it but there was a quote similar to this, "History is always written by the winners with the blood of the defeated". I'm sure I have that slightly wrong, but it is so true. This statement rings so true in American history, as well as the history of the world in general. I wonder who the savages would be if the Native Americans could write American history? This is nothing unique to America, but we sure didn't do much to make it better.

One of the things I learned, as we all did, was the enslavement of black people by the United States. This had also been done throughout Europe, but that trend was kind of on the way out in Europe at the time. This is nothing out of common knowledge, but much of the brutality has been masked and glossed over. The history of our mistreatment of almost all of our minorities has been so much more brutal than anything you are taught in school. It even goes far beyond slavery. And even way beyond the Native American and black communities. The United States was also a little unique in the extent that we used slavery to build our nation. It is argued, and argued well, that the Americas would not have been able to flourish as quickly and greatly as it did if we would have done our own work and not built our prosperity on the enslavement of other people. The United States rose quickly as a global leader because we leaned so heavily on slave labor. The treatment of our slaves was also one of the most brutal examples of the treatment of slaves in history. Slaves would be beaten within an inch of their lives and then left outside to die from the elements just so the owner could not be accused of physically killing the slave. This action came from the biblical commandment in Exodus 21 that if the slave dies right then from the beating, the slave owner would be accused of murder. However, if the slave survived a day or two then the owner was not liable. Much of our brutality towards slaves was grounded in biblical teachings. The female slaves were used as cattle by the landowner to produce offspring so that the landowner would not need to purchase more slaves. In fact many of the landowners raped the female slaves and still used their own children as slaves. If the children did not have "pure blood" in them, they could be enslaved with no acknowledgement of who the white parent was. I know this subject is brutal but needs to be known by the general public regardless of how painful, and what I cover in this book is only the tip of the iceberg! This doesn't hold a candle to the real brutalities. I also know that many will say that slavery is illegal now and the Civil War fixed all this. These type of statements are blatantly false and are normally an intentional effort to bury one's head in the sand and ignore even recent history. I do not wish to paint everyone under too broad of a brush, because some are simply unaware of the true horrors our country took part in.

"You are not to be so blind with patriotism that you
can't face reality…"

~Malcom X~

Many social systems were constructed post Civil War to keep black people subjugated and enslaved for many years, even still today. The practice of city zoning and "red lining" of these cities is a direct result of trying to control and segregate the black population. Many black slaves were used in the rural south. During our major wars such as World War l, World War ll, and Korea there were huge labor shortages in America. Unemployed and impoverished black people from the south flooded to the cities to keep the American economy going. There were jobs a-plenty, and it gave an economic opportunity to the black community that they never had. Housing was provided and constructed in the inner cities that were literally constructed like ghettos, because that's what they were. They didn't want the black population intermingling, so they lured them with housing and sectioned them off. Once the wars were over, the white GI's came back home and wanted their jobs back. New housing developments were built for the GI's. These were nice family homes, and the agreement was literally written in contracts that the homes could not be sold to black people. They then zoned the cities and "red lined" the ghettos and sections where black people were held. No banks were allowed to loan money to the people inside those red lined zones. The black people were fired from their jobs, the businesses moved to different locations and the inner cities were left destitute and impoverished. Prosperous black areas were not tolerated, and some were burned to the ground, such as Tulsa, Oklahoma also known as "Black Wallstreet". White people had such a hatred that a huge race riot was conducted by the white citizens of the city. Some of the white citizens were deputized and arms were distributed. What followed was the destruction of Greenwood through rioting and outright firebombing of the Greenwood district. What we tend to forget is that most of the race riots in this country have been conducted by white people. In recent years we react out of fear and hatred to condemn black protests and riots with complete ignorance that most of history's race riots were conducted by whites out of their hatred for black people. I have even heard some white people say "you don't see any white people out there acting like that" while watching recent protests on TV. The ignorance is astounding. Some of this ignorance is intentional, however most of it is due to a lack of actual and real history lessons. Furthermore, when Black people did attempt to gather peacefully, they were often times shut down violently. Some of the protests that did have aggression was in part due to the immense frustration of not being heard, with some realizing that no one will pay attention unless something drastic is done. One misconception spread by governmental systems and the media was that of the Black Panthers. The Black Panthers were a peaceful organization that, in its early years were strictly focused on social issues. They did exercise their second amendment rights to open carry, after they were met with violence themselves. They often exercised this right to police their own neighborhoods. Many black neighborhoods were continually harassed by police and other government entities. The Black Panthers provided armed escorts for defenseless people who were in danger, such as escorting Malcom X's widow to the airport so that she too would not be assassinated. Many white people still exercise this right to this day by open carrying handguns and even AR-15s. If anyone dares to even make a slightly sideways remark about this, one is criticized very harshly about the right to bear arms and self-defense. Any encroachment on this right by the government would eliminate freedom and plunge us into communism. Well, I am here to remind you that is exactly what happened to black people and members of the Black Panthers. Many Black Panthers and their leaders were ruthlessly murdered by our government, even while sleeping in their beds. These people were often completely innocent wanting only peace and equal rights. Often times the police would kill anyone in the room. Almost every black social justice hero of the past was gunned down in cold blood. This trend continues to this day. I would not be afraid at all to walk down the streets open carrying a handgun. Many black people however have been gunned down just on suspicion of carrying a weapon, or just by walking down the wrong street. So why don't they "protest peacefully?" They have, and still do. Many lost their lives just by speaking up and gaining public attention.

To further exacerbate the problem, there was a law passed very shortly after the civil war that black people could not be used as slaves, except for if they were a criminal and imprisoned. This led to the mass round up of black males, with little to no conviction, where they were once again used as free labor on chain gangs. After many black people were corralled into ghettos, drugs were introduced into the inner cities. With no jobs available and drugs easily accessible, the use of drugs spread quickly. Police forces quickly patrolled the perimeter of these inner cities with most of the people traveling out of these zones being targeted and searched. The prisons to this day are still a "for profit" enterprise that runs much the same way as a hotel does. These are private businesses that get paid to keep their beds full. They quite literally specialize in having "repeat customers" and have absolutely zero intentions of rehabilitating anyone. One of the problems we face in legalizing marijuana is that it would cause a huge dip in revenue for the prison system and the police forces. Furthermore, what would you do with those currently or previously locked up for marijuana? Studies show that the use of drugs today are just as common among the white community as among the black community. The police could feed the prison system just as easily by patrolling and searching those coming out of the golf clubs and universities, but they don't. Wall Street literally has drug dealers in suits and ties with briefcases full of cocaine and are largely ignored. Crack cocaine was specifically introduced into inner cities, and it carries a stricter punishment even though it is only a cooked down version of cocaine. I would also say through personal experience that methamphetamines and heroin run rampant in small towns and rural America, and yet do not get near the attention as the drugs in the inner cities. The drug use in some small towns in America is a flat out epidemic with almost every family being affected by it in one way or the other. I personally know many people who struggled with drug use and hardly any of them did any prison time, even if they were caught with drugs in their possession. This is largely contributed to the fact that they came from "the right side of the tracks". Because I know these people personally, I can also see them for the good people they are. I would never consider them worthy of prison, even though almost all of them have done criminal things to feed their habits. I know some who have stolen from others including family, yet are viewed with compassion. When they are known personally you can see their humanity and continue to see the real person inside of them. You view them more as having an illness that needs to be cured, rather than a criminal that needs to be punished. The thing is that the "drug war" has created way too much money for too many systems in this country. The war on drugs has not worked at all and it will never work. Many know this and yet the drug war rages on because it is too profitable, and it still serves a purpose for controlling the black population of America. These are all manmade and governmental systems, that have been pedaled to us as being necessary and are shut off from questioning. If you really think about it, what does prison really do? I mean I understand if someone is a violent criminal that you do not want them loose on the streets, however taking a drug offender and simply locking them up for ten years as punishment does absolutely no good. Most of the time rehabilitation is not offered and they are placed next to hardened criminals. Many people going in there are simply taught how to be real criminals by the real criminals around them. The system is also so tough that sometimes they need to enter into a dirty system just to survive. Simply locking people up for a predetermined period of time and then releasing them does absolutely nothing to help heal anyone. Many times it just creates a repeat offender, with their names forever tainted on job applications, leaving little choice but to turn to more "criminal" activity. Many people have never given this a second thought because "drugs = bad" and druggies shouldn't be on the streets. Most have no idea that the drug war, prison system, and police force have all been created and used for control and profit. I want to give a disclaimer here. I am not attacking or demonizing police officers or prison guards. This is a critique of the system, not its employees. Most of the employees of these systems are only a product of the systems they serve, with no more knowledge of this than anyone else. Most of these people are very good and passionate people, unaware of how or why the systems were established. We also need to keep in mind, that we are caught up in fighting to uphold the very systems that have created these problems in the first place. Crack cocaine and other drugs were literally introduced into the inner cities and prisons were built left and right with every intention of making money from it. Police officers and even a system for getting real dangerous people off the streets may be necessary, however I do not believe the systems that oppress others are necessary in their current configurations. Like religion, one could very easily argue that these systems have damaged way more people than they have helped. People such as drug users and other non-violent criminals are used as something almost sub-human and the system has no desire and no plans of rehabilitation for these people. Their humanity and state of brokenness is overlooked, and they are viewed as repeat customers and a way to keep beds full. It simply comes down to the belief that these systems are flawed. If they are necessary, then they are not necessary in their current forms.

I have one more point to make on this subject. Even though slavery has been "abolished" after the Civil War, many atrocities were committed for many years afterwards. Many of us know that segregation was a thing, but yet many are unaware of the unimaginable evils that came out of it. Lynching was carried out on a quite regular basis. The way some of them were carried out makes a lion eating its prey alive look like child's play. Some of the most horrible of these happened to young teenagers. The one young man was burned alive in front of a crowd while his attackers were laying claims to bones and such to keep as souvenirs. Post cards would sometimes be made with pictures of the horrendous scenes and sent to family members across the country, much like one would do at a beach vacation. One man sent a picture to his family of the charred remnants of such a scene, and mentioned something along the lines of this being the barbecue they had that day. I hesitate to even write about such barbarism because I am afraid that I am the wrong person to give voice to these things. I just want people to be aware that these things happened, because I sure wasn't. Many of these lynching's took place without due trial and were public spectacles with no consequences to the perpetrators. The details get so grotesque that I do not even feel as though I have the right to speak to them because I am afraid I could not fully do it justice. My suggestion is to have the reader actually look these things up for yourself. These types of things can easily be found through searching public archives. Some of this stuff is not necessarily public knowledge, but lay just under the surface, easily uncovered by anyone willing to look. The thing of it is that lynching and segregation in all its horrible forms happened so recently that it is still in living memory of some alive today. There are examples of all of these horrible things that quite literally happened during the lifetime of people still alive today, with others having direct memory of these things happening. In fact many lynching's happened in private after public ones were frowned upon. On March 21, 1981 Michael Donald, a 19 year old black man was hung from a tree by the Alabama KKK. The details of it are absolutely savage. Multiple people participated in this lynching but only one was executed. It was the only execution of a KKK member in the twentieth century despite the large number of racial murders. When someone makes some statement about the Civil War fixing slavery and that current minorities have no need to pursue justice, it only serves to reveal the level of ignorance still prevalent to this day. Such a person is either extremely ignorant to the facts or is in blatant denial of the truth.

This is a very depressing subject and is no fun to write about because it brings out such darkness in our humanity. We do however need to be aware of these things and know what systems were built around such atrocious evil. We need to remember that people lived these nightmares, the least we can do is honor them and remember the horrible things they endured. I write only briefly about the black history of this nation, and it hasn't even touched the equally sever atrocities committed against the native peoples of this land. Their treatment was just as inhumane, from the outright genocide of their people, to the boarding schools that took many more lives. Many tribes were outrightly gunned down with no survivors left to tell their side of the story. There are pictures of frozen corpses laying in the snow, with the majority of them being the elderly, women, and children. Natives were given disease filled blankets to kill as many off as they could. Boarding schools, made to eliminate native heritage in the Americas killed thousands, and remained open in some ways into the late 1970's. In 1978 the Indian Child Welfare Act was passed that gained native parents the right to not send their children to off-reservation schools. There are still Native Americans alive today that remember the death and horrible conditions of these boarding schools. I believe there can be an inherited trauma that is passed down through generations the same way trauma can be passed from a parent to their children. This can cause a whole people group to guard themselves very strongly against outside influence. The Native Americans would be an example of this. One of the last times Native Americans opened up and welcomed outsiders, it led to the mass genocide and incarceration of their whole people group. Once again, I know I am not doing this justice because the atrocities were so numerous and so horrendous that one would need to devote their career to its research in order to go into more accurate detail. I once again encourage the readers to go investigate for yourselves.

When looking back over the eons of world history, it is very easy to see that it has been a very tumultuous and violent history. There has been war after war, oppression after oppression. There has been so much violence that there has been no time in history that I am aware of that a war of some kind has not been raging. It is my personal belief that one would be very hard pressed to find an instance where a border or social system was not used to justify the oppression and aggression used in any major conflict. We can use a national border to declare exceptionalism just because we were born inside of those imaginary lines. America does it now and many other nations have done, and still do the same. Germany undoubtedly did this during the second world war, and England did this during the Opium Wars in China. Religions declare very similar things just because one shares a common belief. Most of the time this is simply because someone was born inside a certain religious border, the same way one is born into a geographical border. Most religious people in the United States would claim Christianity simply because it is the predominant religion of the area. Christianity and Islam both used the idea of exceptionalism through religion during the Crusades and continue the trend up to present day. Judaism is guilty of the same. I am aware that most other religions of the world are responsible for their own share of "justified" violence, however they are not all equally to blame. The Abrahamic religions or the "big three" tend to take the lion's share. I believe one would be hard pressed to argue otherwise. The "big three" seem to be the most violent of them all as far as body count goes, and that count continues to rise as the days go on. It is ironic, or maybe not at all, that these three (Christianity, Islam, and Judaism) all declare the same God as their supreme being. All three trace their religion back to the God of Abraham. It is my personal belief that the reason why these religions tend to be so popular and predominantly violent is that they can be so easily bent and twisted into almost anything you want them to be. Sure they all teach love and peace, however there is also extreme violence in all of the sacred texts of each religion. Mostly the love and peace part is reserved for people within that particular religion, and the rest of humanity is more or less considered outsiders. This can easily be seen as Christians call the community to "pray for the Christians in…" as other humans suffer equally around them. It is easy to see when, in a disaster area, a group singing hymns is focused on, while people physically working to help others are overlooked. It is extremely easy to take all three Abrahamic religions and use them for evil intent when the religion itself teaches that the only ones who are to be acceptable are the ones within that very religion. All three teach that there will be an extremely violent end for anyone who does not remain within the borders of that specific religion. The ones within that religion are more highly favored by God and the rest of humanity will quite literally be damned. The ultimate judge and executioner of each religion is God himself. So if "our God" is going to damn you to eternal punishment, and currently has a higher running body count than any other being in existence, then it is very easy to justify a holy war of sorts, with anyone outside our religious borders.

During all the wars that America has fought, to bring justice to the oppressed, America itself was oppressing millions of minorities back home and even killing them by the thousands. The overall number of Native Americans and other minorities that were slaughtered is probably impossible to calculate. The systematic ways in which the United States controlled and eliminated its minorities was highly admired by Hitler. He and his party studied the science and tactics behind American oppression and used it to perfect his subjugation of the Jews. The United States' narrative of offering freedom to the oppressed and "liberty to all" is foundationally a lie. If we were honest, it would go more like this, "…with liberty and justice for all… I mean all white people, I mean all Christian European white people, no Chinese or Asians either… No Muslims… I mean only men, women don't have equality either… so yeah, with liberty and justice for all Caucasian Western European Christian men!" I know this sounds harsh, but look back on history and tell me where we have ever truly believed in equality for literally all people. It does not exist.

This is not just a big America bashing fest where I am intending to single out only the Americas. This should be taken in a way that points out the fallacy of governments and nations. If this is the dark underbelly of America, then what could lie under the surface of other nations? If this is the true reality of the land of freedom and prosperity, then what takes place elsewhere? The truth is that when most of today's governments, nations, and overall social systems were established, they cared only about power and prominence. They held very little regard for anyone that was not like them, and they had no problems wiping out whole people groups to get their way. My view of it is that we (society) are existing on systems and structures that are foundationally wrong. The way that America came to be was horribly flawed from the onset. If our very foundations are set in evil and darkness, then are they really serving our best interest? If they are foundationally shaky, then will they eventually come crashing down on their own? If a nation and its religions and so many other things were established on poor moral foundations, then how many systems are equally flawed? Jay Wright Forrester, founder of system dynamics argued that "unsuccessful public policies aim to treat the symptoms rather than the causes of social issues and that they also generally focus on efforts rather than on results. This occurs because there is either an incomplete understanding or a misunderstanding of the causes of an issue on the part of the policymakers, which often leads to ineffective or detrimental policies which aggravate the issues they were implemented to correct, or cause other issues to arise. Another problem

Forrester notes is that some policies which may work in the long run may aggravate an issue in the short term. A successful policy according to Forrester must target the correct leverage points. In this case the aspect of the social problem which, if modified, will produce a sizeable enough effect to correct the problem." https://en.wikipedia.org/wiki/Social_system

He states in one of his lectures that "we are not only failing to solve the persistent problems we face, but are in fact causing them." He also says that systems thinking requires "inquiry skills so that we can uncover our hidden assumptions and biases. …requires understanding that all models are wrong and humility about the limitations of our knowledge." https://Web.mit.edu ~Jay Wright Prize Lecture of 2002~

Our ideas of business, prosperity, and the method in which we pursue them could all be wrong. If our idea of morality comes from a nation and religion built on oppression, then could our view of business, careers, family structures, morality, etc. (which are all influenced by the flawed systems) all be foundationally weak as well? Maybe all of these things do not just need to be thrown into the trash, but maybe we need to seriously re-evaluate these systems and how they function. Is it really important for me to have a nine to five job where I pursue money so that I can own a truck that drives me to work, so that I can own a house, television, phones, lawn mower, tools etc. that all seem to only support my nine to five job? The things we pursue seem to only be things that sustain us in order to survive and serve the system. The toys and gadgets we have, only seem to numb us from the sheer absurdity of dedicating our lives to a company and job that cares little about us. We are more seen as an asset to these systems rather than humans who have a life worth living. Many of us devote our lives to these jobs, so that we can have money to own things that take our minds off our miserable lives, that are made miserable by our jobs and the pursuit of money. It is a viscous circle. Many people live for the weekends so they can go four-wheeling, camping, clubbing, barbecuing, fishing, to sports games and so on. Most of the time they can't wait to go do these things because their lives are miserable otherwise. Our lives are oftentimes made miserable by the systems we have been taught that we so desperately need. I am not even saying there are just a few people in high places that keep us brainwashed and keep pedaling these lies. Maybe some are, but not all. I believe it is more like we live inside a construct of systems that we have collectively developed. Many people, including those in power, may simply be upholding systems that they inherited the same as everyone else. Some of these systems may have been useful in their time. Regardless of their origins, these systems just became a way of life. This is just how it has always been done and we as a society, as a collective species simply haven't questioned it. Maybe we can never fully get away from everything. I mean I do like my house and my air conditioning, but do we really need to go about it this way? Maybe my creature comforts are actually not necessary. Maybe if we lived in more primitive and communal way, more like the native tribes of the world who have been all but eliminated, maybe that lifestyle would actually produce more happiness and comfort. Could it be a mixture of the two?

In the not-so-distant future, hopefully there will be more love that is given, and given more freely due to the lack of personal walls and borders, and through the lack of unnecessary and inherently evil systems. This possibility can only be realized if we start now, knowing full well that we may not get to fully experience this ourselves, but still have a passion to see humanity progress towards a better existence. What better legacy to leave in this existence then to realize that you began a work that enabled generations after you to live in a less painful world?

CHAPTER 10:

WHERE DO WE GO
FROM HERE?

I FEEL LIKE THIS IS the point in the book where I would like to
switch gears. I have spent a lot of time talking about our current
world and the problems I believe I see. My intent for doing that is
not to have yet another book just waylaying on everything around
us. Even though criticism of things is healthy, and I do not necessarily intend to give answers, too much criticism without any reason or
direction is not always helpful. I want to raise questions in people's
mind and hopefully make people aware that there is a different way
of viewing things. Hopefully it will get people to loosen their grip
even slightly in order to open their minds a little more to other possibilities. Once we have done that then we can imagine a different
world. A world that may have a little less subjugation, suffering, and
violence. If we can learn to think outside our given systems then

we can truly take the lids off our imaginations and perceive a new universe. That's where I would like to go from here.

For me, amongst all the craziness today, I still have hope in humanity. I love people and believe we are capable of extraordinary things. I believe that the vast majority of humanity is still good and really wants what is good for other people. We may disagree about what that looks like sometimes, but most of the time we actually want very similar things. I also believe that a lot of people who we consider evil are sometimes simply people who have been misguided or injured by a flawed system that society has created. This is one reason why I have shied away from propping up human made systems such as governments and religion. That's not saying we don't need government of some sort, however I will not prop my government up at the expense of other people. I believe that the quickest way one can make a difference in this world is to focus on improving one's self. I want to be a good parent so my children can be even better than I. They hopefully pass that desire along to their children. Eventually at some point the majority of society is going to get better if everyone just focuses on making themselves a better person and loving well all the ones around them. In the end it really just comes down to caring about people and not caring about manmade systems. Only then can I push for change in an unbiased way that will benefit everyone. Only in that way will our world get better. Politics and government will never make this planet any better. We have been taught that politics and religion are the way to create change, but I believe the complete opposite is true. Only by forgetting these power systems can we focus on what really matters. I think my general view on life as such then becomes my theology (for lack of better terms). I don't hold theology as being scriptural or even pertaining to or being made up of something physical such as a "God Being". The divine (whatever that looks like), I believe put itself into creation, so the substance of "God" is quite literally what is manifest around us. Humanity and the universe around me are quite literally divine. Separation from this divinity would be impossible. I view this divine force as being something like a diamond. All the things that make up the universe including all humans are the essence of this diamond. We are all individual facets of this diamond. The light that passes through this diamond is all refracted and broadcast differently and uniquely through each facet. You cannot separate a facet from a diamond, because the facets, once cut and polished are quite literally what gives a diamond its beauty. To remove a facet from a diamond would ultimately destroy the diamond itself. Once a new human enters this existence, a new facet is cut. Once a facet is cut, it cannot be removed without ruining the whole thing. If you want to connect with the divine essence of the universe, then begin by connecting with what is around you, and what is inside you. It is all part of this diamond. Begin "reading" creation and not a religious text. Creation in all its glory is the true expression of all that is divine with divinity having poured itself out and breathed itself into all that exists. This could give the biblical creation story so much power. Rather than diminishing it to argue a literal creation account that upholds one's religion, it could tell the story of how the divine nature quite literally entered into or was breathed into each person. Divinity is not something separate from you. It IS you. The divine became you. The divine is everything around you. A tree or a butterfly quite literally is a unique expression of what "god" is. So, my views I have of this creation actually become my theology and creation itself becomes my scripture.

I believe that we can begin to stitch together an alternate view of the cosmos only once we see that we have biases and world views that may not hold the ultimate truth. If we hold onto our perceptions too tightly and our world view is distorted, then it will automatically shut down vision and keep our thought patterns too narrow. For instance, if I believe that I am exceptional simply because I prescribe to a certain religion or nationality, then it will be almost impossible to see the true value of others outside of the borders that I live within. If my religion requires me to only accept two options of existence in the afterlife, then my creative imagination on that subject is crippled at best. It will also cause me to scream heresy at anyone who does try to explore further possibilities. A subject that has very little to do with how well a person chooses to live their life will suddenly become a place of division and malice. If you are of the religious persuasion, then please try to see that our brain and imagination has been given to you by your creator and you were created in His image. Your imagination is a reflection of His creativeness. Even if you believe it has been defiled, then you should also believe that it has been redeemed through Christ as well. Also imagine a person living thousands of years ago who had a glorious view of the afterlife or "heaven". What language was available for them to express what they saw? What would have been the ultimate utopian place of existence for that culture and time. Imagine the struggle of trying to convey such a vision to one's contemporaries. Does it mean heaven is really a city with streets of gold and gates made of pearls, or is that what spoke to them in their day? Using your imagination to expand your views of paradise is not a bad thing. Sure, imagination can be used for evil, but it is also the birthplace of all that is good and precious. If you now have the mind of Christ, you have the ability to discern what is good and evil. This is also true if you adhere to the creation narrative. Don't be afraid to imagine. If you will ultimately be redeemed and made perfect when you reach the next realm then would you also not have the power to choose and create the reality in which you would like to live in? I remember back as a Christian that I of course didn't want to go to hell, but my vision of heaven didn't look very fun either. I had a picture of being trapped in a city that had walls and a gate. Even though this city was grand and glorious, I still viewed it as a place that would confine me. I also heard many people say that we will be so enamored with the glory of God that we will spend eternity praising God. This didn't sound much better than the alternative destination if I may be honest. I also think that we need to accept the fact that someone's perception of reality does not need to be everyone else's perception of reality. If sitting around praising God for eternity sounds good to someone then so be it, but it doesn't need to be your reality if you don't like it. No one should force you into viewing things through their lenses. If you find yourself under that kind of "leadership" then please get away very quickly. If you are that type of "leader" then please step down immediately.

On the flip side of this, if you find yourself on the strictly evolutionary side of things with science dictating the reality that you see, please be open minded with people who add different elements into their world view. Maybe consider adding some to yours as well. When you finally have the freedom to ask or ponder the deep hard questions of life outside a certain religious context, things can seem to become very unstable and scary at times. The trick is to keep moving. Keep pressing forward. Do not avoid the tough questions. If an idea or question arises and it scares you or you find yourself shrinking back, ask yourself why you react that way to it. Most often you actually need to dive into it headfirst. Most of the time we become afraid of questions that would shake the foundations of everything we have been taught. One of these questions that I found myself shrinking back from was the question of "creation vs evolution". I was handed the belief that creation was undoubtedly the way that everything came to be. I was also taught that the only way this could be possible was written in a book outlining everything in exact order and it all happened in seven days roughly six thousand years ago. This was taught to me in no uncertain terms. To consider anything different was very taboo to say the least. I have grown to love science and the wonders that it reveals. There is however a fringe element in the scientifically minded that adhere to their scientific "facts" much like the religious community adheres to theirs. Being too focused on the answers of science and only having a world view based on the things that science reveals is also a recipe that can lead to a narrowminded and dogmatic reality. For me to only believe and perceive things based on what science can reveal would be kind of depressing as well. I agree that science allows the use of imagination as to what is physically possible in this universe, but has given me very little satisfaction when answering things that I consider deeper and maybe more fulfilling. Science adds to my imagination of what is possible and can even help shape my ideas of what is possible spiritually, but normally doesn't have the answers that my inner being needs. In short, I believe there is a ditch we can fall into on both sides of the road. You will find very dogmatic people in both ditches, and few people in either ditch are open to outside criticism. If a scientifically minded person is not open to people sensing a reality outside the realm of science, or does not allow for others perceiving a flaw in scientific explanation, coming from a place of one's inner self, then I believe science has become a religion for that person. For some, religion and science have become enemies to each other. Some on both sides of the issue seem to have devoted their lives to using one to disprove the other. Sure science can disprove thing such as Noah's flood story, but in my opinion (pr at least for me) it should not be used as a substitute for spirituality. I fully believe in an inner intuition, or a higher more complete realm of knowing that comes from a place other than our cognitive brain. Maybe there is some exploration into this through quantum science, however I believe this is something science can't begin to explain. There seems to be an element of cosmic existence that science, without some mysticism, cannot begin to touch. In my mind, when it comes to evolution and my existence, there is a mystical side that evolution alone simply cannot explain. I am not outright disputing evolution at all, however I believe that there needed to be a divine interaction somehow and somewhere to create something as beautiful as a human and all that we contain. I fully believe that looking at the wonders of the universe through a strictly scientific view simply falls way short of the majesty of it all. For me to believe in evolution and the universe coming into existence in a purely scientifical way without divine intervention would be just as tasteless and oversimplified to me as believing in a literal creation narrative as described in the bible. To me they both seem to fall way short of the true wonderment of everything. To me, both should be combined into one harmonious thing that can provide real nourishment for the soul. My view on things, however, should never be used to claim any ultimate truth. My perception of things may be completely different than someone else's. Maybe someone has absolutely no interest in science and others no interest in religion. That is completely fine, but I would refrain from discrediting those who love both.

One more place I would like to touch on is Atheism. I want to say that this opinion of this subject is not meant to paint atheism into a corner. I have listened to many deep and brilliant atheists, and some have a wonderful outlook on the universe. As I mentioned earlier in the book, I do not fully disagree with atheism and think that atheism has a lot of strong qualities. I know I am speaking of atheism as if it was a religion. I realize that many claim that it is not a religion, and I would agree that if used in its basic form it would not be a religion. Buddhism also claims it is not a religion, and I have heard Christians claim that Christianity is not a religion. I also want to reiterate that I actually blame Christianity and the Abrahamic religions for most of the world's atheists. That is not implying anything against atheists, it is simply my belief that most atheists are running from a Christian God more than anything. I get it because so am I. It is my personal belief that many people were only given one option of god to believe in, and that was the Christian god Yahweh. There are very limited ways you can look at a divine being if Yahweh is the only option that you have. Since Yahweh and his portrayal in Christianity is repulsive, those leaving Christianity simply chose not to believe in any god at all. For many, I don't think they really even knew there was a different way of looking at spirituality and simply tossed it out. I sure didn't know there were different options. I also think that if anyone went through religious trauma, and that trauma was their "push" out of Christianity, the idea of rebuilding a new spiritual outlook would appear rather daunting and even flat out repulsive. Trust me, I understand. Since at one time there were very few options outside of Christianity in the Western world, atheism just kinda seemed like the place to go. I believe atheism is a very necessary thing to have for many people. It is a place to go to unwind and just forget about religion. It is a place to go to heal from religion and simply focus on one's existence in the here and now. A place to just chill. When someone sits in a place that is quiet enough for long enough, the mind will become restless, and the soul starts searching. Searching for a meaning to life and searching for significance from a place of being atheistic can be a bit dark for some people. Once again, I know this isn't the case for everyone. I also know that some atheistic people get very defensive of atheism when it is criticized or questioned. Some people in atheism become very dogmatic and essentially turn their beliefs inside atheism into a religion of sorts. As such, I have heard some people attempting to make sense of everything from inside atheism. Some have become so set in upholding atheism that they go about defending it much the same as a Christian apologist would. The claim that one should only live from what they can perceive in front of them and only believe in what can be proven is very similar to scientifically minded people who only believing in what science can prove. There are many things in the intuitive and mystical world that science cannot prove, and shutting one's self off from that realm, in my opinion, is only allowing yourself to live from half of who you truly are.

If you are waiting to move out into the world of imagination and spirituality only after it can be proven, then you will probably reach the end of your life in the same place you are at presently. Our physical senses and science will probably never (or at least not in our lifetimes) be able to prove divinity or the realm of spirituality. I could be wrong and would love to have to "eat my hat" on this one, but I do not see spirituality as something that science can prove. Seriously, I hope someone says, "hold my beer" and legitimately proves me wrong. I believe this spiritual realm is largely untouched and remains open for exploration.

I also believe that religion has also tainted the word "god" for a lot of people. I believe many people who have been repulsed by religion find themselves equally repulsed by the word "god." God has been used as such a sledge hammer that a lot of "de constructed" people want nothing to do with the word. I find myself trying to find adequate words for divine power, essence, and presence. I do not believe this to be some single physical or spiritual entity. I keep trying to express it in a different way, however even our language is limited to our past and the religious systems that dictated it. I feel as though I want to refer to this divine nature that flows through all that exists as something different than just "god." I even feel as though that one single word as it has been previously defined, simply falls short. It almost seems that a new spiritual language needs to be developed, because I find myself confined by traditional terms. Some spiritual practices that rely on meditation and deep quiet reflection may have begun to dip their toes into this other world. I do however believe that if someone approaches it from a thing even such as Buddhism, you are still kind of limiting yourself to certain borders and boundaries in order to stay within the Buddhist (or whatever labeled entity) ways of doing things. The same with Hinduism and yoga. Does this even make sense to anyone other than me? I feel a lack of words to describe what I am trying to say. In my mind, it is something that should be explored with as little labeling as possible in order to keep the exploration as limitless as possible. Trust me, I am still not there either. I just have a vision inside me of where I want to go, and I am still very much in the discovery stage of this. This however is the point from which I want my imaginative exploration to begin.

CHAPTER 11:

PREVIOUS HUMAN EXPERIENCE

SOMETIMES MY BRAIN SEEMS TO focus on the physical world and our systems that we find ourselves in, but what about the spiritual side of things? What about the afterlife or next realm of existence? Is there such a thing? If there is then what does it look like? This is a subject that has been heavily debated, and there are many ideas as to what the next life might be. There are some possibilities that look attractive and some that do not. There are strengths and weaknesses to them all. Some sound very desirable from an afterlife perspective, but do not help out much with how we live our lives here and now. I would like to take a bit of time to talk about the different perspectives.

Is this life that we are living now our only human experience? Have we had a human experience in a previous life? Will we have future human experiences?

My career requires me to drive a lot. I drive from city to rural, flatlands to hill country. Sometimes I find myself in inner cities and from there I may head out to Amish country. Sometimes I drive through an area that tugs at the heartstrings of my soul so much that I could almost get emotional, even though I am normally even keeled when it comes to showing emotion. I had this happen about a week ago where I was driving through some countryside. It was a nice stretch of land, but nothing that out of the ordinary. Suddenly out of nowhere I found myself staring at this ridge and hillside draped in a forest of trees with an open field below it. Something hit me in my memory bank, or my subconscious made its way to my conscious brain or something. I felt strongly as if I recognized it. I don't just mean a small tinge of deja vu, but a serious blow in my thoughts and feelings, in my soul. I suddenly felt such a strong feeling of nostalgia and a longing for that place. It took me so by surprise that I almost had to pull over, wondering what the heck just happened. It was as if my inner being was having a memory of a previous life, as if taking a stroll down memory lane. It was as if I drove past a childhood home, and it was beckoning me, as if I had a physical connection to the place. I even had a tinge of sadness as if I had also experienced some form of hard times and pain at this place. It is almost as if my soul or sub conscience has a connection to that place, as if one were to walk through a childhood home, remembering all the good times as well as very sad times. It is almost as if the place or region caused my very inner being to recall a very ancient memory of the area and I became homesick. I know this may sound strange, and it sure was strange to me. I never felt anything like that so strongly. But how can this be if I have never seen that place before? How could I have such a connection to a place that I have never lived at before?

Usually when my mind thinks about things such as the possibility of multiple human experiences, it runs off into a hundred different bunny trails. The thought of having to do this whole human thing again and again can get a little heavy, and darn near depressing sometimes. I am by no means depressed nor do I wish to leave this existence early, but…again?!? This life has been hard. I'm not old by any stretch, but yet sometimes I just feel tired and wore out already. It's been a tough journey so far. I mean sure it has been fun and rewarding as well but I'm not so sure I wish to do this over. I like the idea of a utopian paradise after my eyes close for the last time on this earth. It's kinda like a "get out of jail free card". The doors are flung open, and you get to go do as you please with no heartache or pain, right? Well, I still don't believe that either even if we never have to be "human" again. I would still like to think that when I'm in the "ever after" and my emotions get to be too much or the pain too heavy that I'll at least be able to go chill on the dark side of the moon for a couple of eons and watch the stars go by. I mean to me that sounds better than a perpetual existence on this planet. The thought of doing this again doesn't seem very attractive at the moment, but could I be missing something? Is there something that I'm not seeing? Even though it may not sound that great now, the idea of it has the capability of urging me to live differently here and now.

If we do have to do this whole "human" thing again, do we get to have a reprieve for as long as we like? Do we get to catch our breath before we do this again? Do we get an intermission that lasts as long as we need it to? Maybe there is still a "place of rest" so to speak. Maybe we can go check out far off galaxies until our souls are drawn back to this big blue planet. Maybe there is something here that beckons our souls, kinda like a home that calls us back. Is there something here that I am missing? Is there a reason why I am drawn back to this place the way that a monarch butterfly is summoned to fly from the far reaches of Canada all the way down to Mexico? Is there an interconnectedness even with a butterfly that brings it back to the same forest from thousands of miles away, generation after generation? Do we have the same kind of pull to this planet that a salmon has, that causes it to find the same stream, the same birthing grounds that gave it life? Maybe we have the same connection to this planet and even specific places on this planet? If so, then to what end? Could being human actually be the most divine state of existence? Will we do this perpetually for eternity? Is there a common goal that we as a collective being are working towards? Is there something here in a common and shared goal that pulls us back time and again? Could this goal, one which our spirit mind is aware of, be the thing that makes this repeated human experience all worth it? Are we as a collective striving to not just heal humanity, but also this planet and all of creation? Is society and this universe evolving forwards towards an existence free of corruption and decay? Could we all be pushing for an existence so whole and well that being here as human could actually be the utopia that we all yearn for? Could heaven only be attained after we create it? A place free of nationality. A place free of wealth at the expense of another's poverty? Could the idea of lack actually be a lie that we have all bought in to? Could we reach a place where we are so self-aware in our ability and power that we could literally create anything we wanted? Is our evolution as a species simply a progressive awareness of our true capabilities? Could we reach such a state of being where all selfishness and hate would cease to exist? All of our focus could be on wholeness as a group, not as an individual. Could we have the potential to be so powerful that I could in fact go check out a distant star if I wished? Could the universe be our playground sometime? Could you imagine being able to quite literally go anywhere you wished for as long as you liked? Maybe being human is more divine than any other state of being, and could actually unlock the door to endless possibilities. Maybe in each human existence we move the ball forward, bit by bit. What if in the next dimension, after we have had our intermission and had a chance to see the end goal, and we see the work our fellow beings are accomplishing, we decide to come back and help move it another inch. We make idealistic statements about leaving the planet a better place, but it never seems to truly motivate anyone very much. We often say that we want to leave this planet a better place for our children. We don't want them to deal with the same stuff we had to deal with. That is an excellent idea, but never seems to bring about any action. Maybe we also need to strive to leave this planet a better place for ourselves when we return. This may motivate people to do something. It'd be kinda nice if I'm going to do this again, if it could suck just a little bit less next time. Do you want to come back in a place full of division, war, and disease? Maybe the idea of coming back as a wealthy American doesn't seem so bad, but what if you would come back as an impoverished person in India, Africa, or the Middle East? Would you still agree with our foreign policy if you had to be on the receiving end of it? Would you agree with our military actions if you came back in Afghanistan? Would you still agree with hoarding wealth if you had to starve in Somalia on the next go around?

Maybe returning here over and over again has a more personal purpose. Maybe this earth and this realm is a place of refinement. Maybe each time you get to come back with your same personality, and every time you do come back you can improve yourself until you meet a certain goal? Would you start taking self improvement more seriously? Would you want to come back and deal with the same issues you have now? Would you be willing to come back and be the same angry person again? Would you hang onto your hatred, depression, anxiety, etc...? Would you want to come back to yet another nine to five job? Would you learn to love more? Would you want to cherish your loved ones more? Would you be kinder to nature? What if you were to have the possibility of coming back as an animal? Would you want to come back as a North American animal that would get hunted every year? Being a deer, elk, or bear could seem to be very fun, but making it to old age without getting shot may be hard to do. Would you come back as an animal in India and have to deal with the horrible garbage and pollution that spills out everywhere? If you came back as a dog in America or as a dog in the East could mean two very different things. In some places a dog can have a very good life, in some places you could be dinner, and in others you get kicked into the gutter to die from starvation and disease. It could be like a game of Russian Roulette. Maybe you have to come back as the thing you hate or disrespect the most. If you are an abuser, what if you had to come back as the abused? Now that would be scary, being the victim of your very own abuse. If we thought like this, we would make friends with our enemies very quickly. We would look at everything through much kinder eyes.

If your beliefs tell you to believe in some other form of after-life, it is still healthy to realize that no one knows for sure. The bible is very vague on an afterlife, and most of us are just running on faith so-to-speak. It would be worth giving these ideas a thought and live as though they were possible. Maybe experiencing this realm as human and animal is all part of it. Maybe experiencing all of this from multiple human perspectives and from animal perspectives rounds out our existence. Seeing things from both the top and the bottom could really make a difference. Maybe this is what refines us and allows us to change our eternal perspective. I don't know what it all entails but revisiting this place does have some strengths even if it does not appear glamorous to me right now.

CHAPTER 12:

THE SOLACE
OF ATHEISM

So, I WANT TO BE careful here. I do not want to talk of atheism as a religion, although at times it may sound like I am. I also do not want to paint it with a broad brush and paint all atheists under the same color, because the thoughts and views among the community are so diverse. I have met and conversed with many atheists who vary from being very deep in their thought and still retaining a sense of spirituality, to those who seem to have had their fill of religion and all spirituality and seem to shy away from anything that goes more than skin deep (which I understand). I am also aware that for the majority of my life I was raised in Christianity and was taught that atheism was demonic and anti-God. I realize that because I have had this conditioning and even though I believe I have shed these biases as much as possible, I am aware it is impossible for one to shed them all and I probably hang on to some that I am not even aware of. Please forgive me if this comes through. I really do not intend to be insulting. I will also say that I have more in common with some atheists that I have talked and listened to than the Christianity of my past. I do not consider myself an atheist at the moment because I still adhere to some form of a higher power, just not a Zeus like god of the bible. Sometimes I feel as though I need a deeper understanding of atheism, because maybe some would consider me to be one. If I would be considered one however, it would back up my idea that a lot of atheists are just atheistic against a biblical type of god and not all divine higher powers of some other kind. I also shy away from leaving one label just to have another slapped onto me. Labels are often used so that others can simply place you in a box and ignore you if they do not like what you have to say. I definitely know that as a Christian I did this often. I sought to label so that I could figure out how I was to take them or judge what they had to say. If someone was labeled as an atheist (or anything other than Christian), I felt as though I had every right to place them in a box, shove them to the side, and not listen to anything they had to say, regardless of how logical they were. I also realize that even though I do not wish to belittle anyone, the very act of talking about different groups is in a way applying a label. Anyways, this has been a long rabbit trail to give the reader a little of my background here before I get into anything.

There is also the idea that atheism is a place one can go in order to carry out a sinful lifestyle. I have heard Christians say things something like "If I didn't have Christianity I don't know what I would do". They said this in a way that meant they wouldn't trust themselves. They would cheat on a spouse or cause harm to themselves or others. If your religion is the only thing holding you together in that way, then you need to find help. It also signifies your religion's inability to bring true healing and true change. If you have truly healed, if you have truly changed, then your good and wholesome lifestyle should simply happen because it's who you are. It should not happen because a book or religion requires it from you. If you let go of your religion and you act in a harmful way then your religion only masked the real problems. Your religion didn't fix anything. More than likely if this is the case, these problems will continue to fester and rise to the surface anyways. Your religion will be unable to hold it back forever. If you allow something to remain in your heart, then no amount of religion can keep you from acting on it at some point in your life. Evil comes from the heart and if you continue to hold evil in your heart even as a religious person, that may be a sign of the inability of that religion to deal with evil. If your religion is truly more powerful than evil, it should be able to remove it from your heart.

Atheism and the view of an afterlife, or maybe the absence of it, varies greatly. As I stated earlier, there are many beliefs inside atheism. I find however that many do not believe in an afterlife. Some are rejecting the religious view of an afterlife, while others are convinced by evidence, and therefore, lacking any evidence of an afterlife they do not believe in one. I do not wish to paint all atheists as damaged people running from the pain of a religious system. Like I just mentioned, some are there due to how their reasoning works. They are moved by what they can see, feel, taste, and physically prove the existence of. If there is no proof, they do not believe. Many are open to the possibility of a higher power and an afterlife, they are just unsure, and are open to evidence. When reasoning with atheists in this position, simply going back to scripture and providing evidence in that way (because the bible says) serves as no evidence at all, and I would agree. Many open minded atheists have searched and read texts of all kinds to explore different possibilities. Some know these religious texts better than the believers of the texts, and see no logic in them. Once again, I agree. Some would even desire a higher power and an afterlife but are not willing to believe in one just yet. This may border on agnosticism, but let's not get too technical.

On the other end of the spectrum, we of course have those who were damaged by religion and are simply done with it. I don't want to spend much time on this one, simply because I feel for those in this category, probably because I can relate so much. I do not wish to cause further damage or pain through further mis-labeling and appearing as though I know all about it. One thing I will say though is that many in this camp come from fundamental religions, probably many from the Christian side of things. Many grew to see the god of the bible and the religion encompassing this deity as monstrous. I would agree here as well because, so do I. Some in this camp may not have considered a different way of viewing divinity and a higher power. Some may have given it thought but simply find the thought undesirable or too exhausting to pursue. I can relate to this. Some here have found atheism as a nice quiet place of respite where they can regroup and simply focus on the present. The thought of worrying about anything outside of the here and now can cause heavy anxiety to some. For that reason and for these people in particular, I have grown to look at atheism with fondness. I look at atheism as a very necessary place that can welcome the broken and just give them a place to exist without the pressure to be something other than themselves. Some may make their home here because of the comfort they found here. Some may use it as a travel plaza that offers rest and refreshment before moving on with their journey. In this sense and through this view, I can see atheism as being a more divine place than most of the world's religions. When atheism takes people just as they are, without hesitation and without judgement, it is doing what many religions claim to do, but consistently fail to do. I would compare this to an experience I had a while back. I was at a home and garden show. The company I worked for had a booth there that I was running, and I went to grab some lunch. The facility was huge and was also hosting a comic-con. I found myself eating lunch among a bunch of people in cosplay. I was the only "business" looking person in the crowd. At first, I wondered if I should go elsewhere, but decided to stay. As I got my food and sat down, I realized that no one there gave a rip about me not looking like one of them. They were all uniquely dressed, and each person brought their unique personality. Uniqueness was embraced and even expected. Where else could you feel more at ease than in a crowd of people comfortable with being unique? As I sat there and looked around, I saw people of all different types, all having a great time together. I had never felt so comfortable and un-judged as I did for those thirty minutes I spent there. It is a memory forever etched into my brain that I hope no senility will ever erase. It was also a critical time in my journey to learn to not look at "weird" people so much differently. I like to think of atheism much like the environment I experienced at that comic-con. A place where people of all different kinds can just come and fit in.

Most atheists I would assume, have a view that an afterlife does not exist. Once again I know there are wide ranges of ideas out there within atheism, however most atheists I have heard on the subject seem to think there is none. Some have expressed the openness and desire to believe in an afterlife, but for whatever reason see no compelling reason to do so. For others, coming to the end of this life and simply being able to fall asleep into nothingness doesn't seem that bad to them. I mean who doesn't like to sleep, right? I have heard one argument that asks what it was like to live during an event before one's life, such as the great depression. Of course the answer would be, "I have no idea. I wasn't alive then." To which the reply would be, "Exactly, that's what it would be like after you die as well." They do have a point there. It's not like it would be horrible. You quite literally would have no consciousness of anything. I know for some the idea of not existing is a scary thought, but it is just that, the thought that is scary. Not existing would not be horrible or scary because you quite literally would not know that you don't exist anymore. You're just... gone. This for some people may actually be a welcoming thought, especially if one has had a rough go at it here on earth. It may be similar to a stay at home parent in a house full of rowdy kids. All you want to do at the end of the day is to go shut your brain off and go to sleep. Sometimes that's all you have energy for, and you don't even have the energy to consider anything else. I can understand that.

I want to interject here a bit and talk about certain atheists that I have read and listened to on various platforms. I have noticed that there is a fringe of atheism that gets rather dogmatic and also opens atheism up to a bit of criticism. I have heard some lash out hard against anyone not believing similar things as they do and calling people silly for having faith in something that has no direct physical evidence of its existence. For instance, I have heard some say that the belief in an afterlife is silly and nonsensical. Some say the belief in an afterlife is only because one is scared of death. I have heard the same said about belief in a higher power. I have had some "run ins" with some who will become very dogmatic in their beliefs the same way fundamental religious people will become dogmatic in their beliefs. They become so focused on attacking fundamental religions and the damage they've created, and do not realize they are doing the same things. We humans realize that things such as oxygen, the air we breathe, and other gasses are real because we can feal the wind blow, we can hear it, and science has proven its reality. Protons, electrons, photons, energy waves, etc., are all real, but to our physical senses, it is as if they do not exist. There are other unseen forces that can be felt, heard, and generally sensed by the soul that some feal are every bit as real as the air we breathe. To some, there are spiritual correlations or connectedness between the observed and the unobserved universe. In other words, there are things in the physical world that would be mirrored in the spiritual, also referred to as "types and shadows." Our physical senses do not necessarily paint a whole picture of reality. Sometimes what we physically perceive isn't reality at all. Looking at solid structures around us may not be that solid at the molecular level, or possibly not even being held together by any known force. Look no further than the quantum world for this. Science may never be able to prove the spiritual realm, however science should never completely undermine the personal senses and our personal experiences. Maybe the spiritual and the scientific world could merge somehow? I believe this was attempted to a small degree in the hippie movement in the 60s-70s, but the world and our development may have not been ready for that either.

Dogmatic atheists can give atheism a bad name the same way any dogmatic person can devalue any other type of religion or group. I know atheism is not a religion, but there is a reason why some believe that it is. I've even heard some of these atheists declare that they are not just atheistic against Christianity, however when they make the claims of the belief in the afterlife as being silly, I feel as though the only view of an afterlife that they reject is a Christian one. I get the sense that if these same atheists were to converse with many indigenous peoples around the globe, and discuss their ideas of the afterlife, they would be very respectful and never call it silliness. I may be wrong, but it's the way I've seen it portrayed. I understand that Christianity leaves itself wide open for criticism, and I most definitely have been critical of it, however it may be more tactful to refine or narrow down one's beliefs a bit. What I mean is to maybe not just reject all beliefs in an afterlife in one broad stroke (unless you have examined at least the majority of them), but rather define what aspects of certain views of the afterlife that you reject. Rather than just broadly rejecting any higher power, one could get more specific as to what type of higher power one rejects. It is also helpful to remember that often times a whole religion and every one of its beliefs cannot just automatically be thrown out. Every religion on earth has its strong points. Not everything that any religion believes is useless garbage. There are viewpoints within them all that are worth retaining or at least being open to. Painting the view of the afterlife with such a broad brush as only limiting it to Christianity, limits the ability to see all of the finer and nuanced beliefs in the afterlife. Many spiritual traditions believe in an afterlife, and some of these views are beautiful. Dogmatism in a sense causes the same narrow mindedness to the atheist as dogmatism causes inside any religion. It cuts one off from outside perspectives and limits one's ability to imagine something bigger and better. Dogmatism will cut you off from conversations and groups that one may benefit from. I just saw an atheist on a social media platform that makes a conservative or Christian statement (pretending he/she is a conservative Christian), then waits to see who likes or agrees with the statement, to which this person quickly "unfriends" or blocks these people. This person will also blatantly say that he/she is trying to rid their friends list of all conservatives and Christians, often mocking them as he/she does so. This is the type of dogmatism that hurts atheists in general. This person is also one of the hosts of a podcast, and they probably do not realize that they are limiting their audience base by doing such outrageous things. I sure know it is why I no longer listen to this podcast, because it reminds me of the dogmatic religion that I left. Dogmatism on such a grand scale is repulsive no matter where it comes from. I do not understand why, if you believe you have something so important to share to the world, why one would automatically limit their audience base so quickly. If you wish to change a society with your insight, do not block the very people you wish to impact. It is as if some people only want to converse with people of a similar mind. If you dogmatically write it all off with one fell swoop, then you have just created another religious doctrine. You may not see the possibility of an afterlife or a higher power now, but by taking such a dogmatic stance on anything, you limit how openminded you can be to the possibility in the future. People who make such bold and absolute claims can sometimes find themselves defending these claims just for the simple fact that they do not wish to look foolish or appear Janus faced. This is exactly what dogmatic religious people do, then spend their time defending the claims they shouldn't have made to begin with.

Having said all of that, there is a majority of atheists who are very deep thinkers and open to new ideas and possibilities. Some people coming from a religious background do find the thought of not having an afterlife as being something super scary. However, the lack of an afterlife does not take away the value of human existence. For some people however, the idea of no afterlife is scary because they want to mean something, and the lack of an afterlife, to some, would take that meaning away. They want their life's work to have value. Some would think that a view of nothingness after death would devalue them and anything they do, because to a lot of these, the afterlife is the exact thing that gives this life any kind of meaning. This was my exact stance on this subject for many years. At one time, I could not see how life could mean anything if we were finite creatures. This subject alone is one of the reasons why I started seeking out atheists. I wanted to truly sit and hear them out to see why they were "ok" with no afterlife. To see so many people holding an atheistic position meant there had to be validity to it, with sound reasoning behind it. I learned something. I found that the lack of afterlife and the lack of meaning do not go hand in hand. The idea associated with the lack of meaning probably signifies that a person has only considered one side of the argument and has not truly heard the outlooks of many atheists. That is not meant to criticize those who have not talked to atheists. I know that for a long time, I had very little interaction with atheists simply because I came from a place with few of them around me. Also in Christianity, Atheism = evil, so one was to guard their hearts and stay as far away as possible. You know, ignorance in the name of self-preservation and polarization. I also believe there is an agenda coming from organized religion to paint atheists as people without meaning, as essentially hollow shells walking around without direction. This life can still have plenty of meaning and people can still have tremendous value if you do not believe in further existence beyond this life. The view of no afterlife has the ability to pull one into the present in a very unique way. One would realize that this life is really all you've got. If you want to experience joy and happiness, then you had better figure out how to do that. One would need to figure out what joy and happiness really mean. One would truly have to figure out how to find joy and happiness rather than shrugging it off and believing true joy is only to be attained in the "ever-after." If you would want to experience true happiness, you wouldn't just "settle for less" because you would be truly aware that this short life on earth is all you have. In one's pursuit of happiness and joy, one would ultimately be led to love, and would be able to display that love very well. No strings attached, just love for the sake of love. To be a good person and to have that legacy live on in the minds of those remaining here is meaning enough. After all, to love and help another without the idea that it will somehow be repaid or benefit you in the next life, is the most pure and unselfish love there is. It may even have more meaning this way. An atheist who is determined to live their life fully in the short time they have available, can give this life and the meaning of it much thought. This person can "give it all they have" in the truest sense of the phrase, because they don't get any more than this life. There are many atheists who are open to an afterlife, but simply say we cannot be sure, and this is absolutely true. This causes a focus on being present, and a living in the moment mentality that is hard to find anywhere else. More people, including myself, need to learn how to be more present with our children, with our partners, and with creation itself. We need to learn how to shrug off the petty things that society can push onto us. We need to take unimportant expectations off of our children and loved ones. We need to enjoy the here and now. Joy is not found in yesterday or tomorrow. Joy is only experienced in the present.

In short, atheism can come up with some very deep (and may I say spiritual) insights. If you experience love from such a person, then you get to experience love in its raw and pure form. It is a love without agenda. You are loved simply because someone cares. How great is that!

I actually believe that religions around the world could learn from this. The teaching that true happiness and a new earth is something that can only be attained after this life, and after this world has been destroyed, has done horrible damage to society in my opinion. It has caused people to give up on world peace and has caused many in my country to focus on short term political goals. Many newly introduced policies would actually deplete society and this earth of resources more quickly than before, all for short term benefits. Candidates are picked because of what they can offer in four to eight years. Normally policies and agendas with short term goals are focused on, with little thought as to how to propel humanity forward in the long term. Long term in today's politics and world views rarely go beyond fifty years, if that. Many religious people from my background do not think that earth will be around in another hundred years, let alone a thousand. Why envision long term solutions for humanity if it's all going to burn soon anyway? At the same time most of the highly political are always focused on the next election cycle, scheming and ever fearful of the damage the opposing party may do if elected. Many only want to know how to push their political agenda for four more years, stuck in a vicious cycle of anxiety and demonization of the oponents.

CHAPTER 13:

HELL

(Don't worry this will be short… kind of… maybe ;-)

WHAT IS HELL? DOES HELL exist? If hell does exist, does it match the modern Christian definition we have been given? Does one pass through hell in this life or the afterlife? To be honest, I almost left the hell issue completely out of this book. I am so over the whole "hell" debate and whether it exists. I have laid this issue to rest inside of me a long time ago. I know other religions teach a hellish type of place, but most are the Abrahamic religions, or come from their influence. Once again, Christianity is what I know and where I come from. That is why I "pick on it" throughout this book. To think of a hell the way modern Christianity teaches it is almost a foreign concept to me anymore. I cannot imagine still living my life wrapped up in this crazy belief system. The thought that an eternal creature's entire existence is based on 80 years in this earth is absurdity in my opinion. Furthermore, if fear of hell is the only reason for staying inside any religion, then this is a direct reflection of how weak the religion is. It also shows that being Christian can be akin to being in an abusive relationship. There is no real love and you're only staying so you don't get your teeth kicked in. Sorry if this triggers people who suffered from physical abuse, but in reality, hell is portrayed as being much worse than anything experienced in this life. The teachings of this place have done the emotional equivalent of physical abuse to many. The correlation between abuses needs to be brought to light. The idea that the worst damage or pain one can experience is in the physical side of things is simply not true. Emotional and spiritual trauma are often way worse than physical trauma. It becomes even more crazy when the very religion that teaches hell the most, claims you cannot see the world and existence clearly as they truly are while in this life. It is a teaching of a "veil" of sorts remains over the eyes in this life. This once again forces humanity into making an eternal decision without knowing the full consequences, just like the "original sin" teaching. This once again teaches a dishonest and sly God, almost tricking people into a torturous afterlife rather than saving us from it. This once again makes the "serpent" look like a rather innocent creature. I absolutely do not believe in hell or this god at all. I have so firmly laid it to rest that in order to debate its nonexistence I would almost have to retrain my brain in the proper thought pattern to do so, and I have zero desire to go there. So do I believe in hell in the traditional way? No, absolutely not. If there is some version of a hell, then I believe everyone is going.

Passing through "hell" could simply burn and strip away all the negative baggage and nastiness that is connected to us. It could be more of a place of refinement. It would be more of a forest fire or a "controlled" burn that gets rid of unwanted vegetation. It would burn over us as if we were a barren landscape with only dried up weeds and unproductive vegetation. The fire could be more cleansing and burn all of that away, and in doing so, it would return all of the nasty unproductive things back to fertile soil. There the soil has a chance to break down these materials into nutrients. Now the soil being clear and healthy again, gives space for new things to grow. The soil has been rejuvenated, giving all the good and new plants the perfect opportunity to flourish like never before. A fire ravaged landscape is often green and lush in only a matter of weeks. This still portrays hell as a physical place and a literal fire, which of course I would not hold to, nor would it be a place of perpetual existence. This is for analogy's sake only.

So, is hell real? Maybe. I believe that IF it is, we must all go there as a place of refinement. I do not believe that any religion could save you from it. I believe hell, if it exists is something that we must all pass through. I do not believe that there is some separate place called "hell", but maybe rather something we could all go through at various times. People willing to face their "demons" could go through it at any time. Those experiencing loss could be going through it right now. Some delaying the dirty work of refinement in the here and now, those who are waiting on heaven to relieve them of this current existence may need to pass through it in the next dimension. Maybe rather than hell being something that we can be spared from, hell may be a thing no one can avoid. Hell, patiently waiting for those choosing to pass through in order to reach paradise on the other side.

I believe that most religions are more like a bad drug that enables you to escape the real issues in front of you. We could compare religion to a person who has been through a very rough time in life, and their escape is turning to drugs. Now in a sense you could say that in the short term, the drugs served their purpose in keeping the person alive in the short term. Drugs can give an otherwise suicidal person a place of escape, and thereby preserving the dependents life for a short time. Drugs are undoubtedly a coping mechanism, and they can work, but only for a short while.

~ **I am by no means advising the use of drugs for anyone. That is absolutely not my intent. I am not a professional by any definition. If this is to be used in any way, let it remove the shame and guilt from people who have already turned to drugs in order to survive, in order to make life bearable. Guilt and shame will only keep a person bound. Do not feel guilty for doing what was necessary to keep yourself alive! Please attempt to move beyond drugs and find a way to heal without them. ~**

The thing with these drugs is that if they remain the only place of escape and serve as a permanent reprieve from reality in order to survive, they will ultimately lead to your demise as well. If one must turn to drugs (which I in no means am condoning or recommending) then let us please not pass judgment, but rather recognize that for some, this was a move necessary for survival. The point, however, should be to move beyond the need for drugs by learning how to process through our grief in a healthy way. I believe that this is almost exactly how the "Abrahamic Religions" work as well. They offer a place of respite for a short time. You actually can gain a sense of a euphoric high for a time through these religions. Many people who leave the church speak about how much they like "praise and worship" inside the church. This is something Christianity has figured out very well. Even though the almost euphoric high that some experience during it is something that comes from within, and anyone can access it at any time, Christianity has learned how to bring it out more easily and consistently. It is very good at setting the mood, creating the atmosphere, and has figured out music in a way that draws it out. Many have discovered ways of accessing this euphoria by using other practices, but yet talk about how easily Christian "praise and worship" can draw it out. It can truly be powerful. It is something that many come back to every week just to experience this high, and care little about the sermon. I have even heard some call it their "drug". I would say two do the same thing. It helps in the short term and can be used effectively. It can be used as a place of escape and a re-energizing of sorts, a place to find one's center, in order to have energy and clarity to do the real dirty work of actively healing. It should not be used as a tool to ignore underlying issues, surviving from one worship service to the next. In my case, after a period of several years I realized that there was no actual solution or healing to my soul. I had to return back to churches and groups for the next high. I pursued the next great thing over and over again. I was promised that "revival" was always right around the corner. I realized, just like a drug, that my highs were never getting me as high and were never lasting as long as the first ones did. I realized that my pursuit was always after the next great thing and kept me distracted from the real problems. The real problems were always under the surface of myself. I needed to stop using religion as a crutch, waiting on god to fix my problems. I needed to snap back into reality and face my "demons" in order to reach a place of peace, joy, and satisfaction that I needed. These were all things that my religion promised me, but always fell short on delivering. Hell, the one thing that religion promised to spare me from was actually the one thing that I needed. In my journey to gain my inner quiet, I actually needed to stop avoiding hell, but actually needed to walk straight into it.

Saying that we need to walk through hell is in no way implying that to suffer some tragic loss or deal with a horrific disability or anything horrible, is somehow a good thing. It is also not implying that some omnipotent god or the universe causes this to happen "for your good". Life somehow automatically seems to present us with enough hardships all on its own. Humanity has created enough evil that we all get to experience our fair share of it. What I am saying is that hell or the process of walking through it normally starts after a significant event, or possibly the building up of a series of events, that ultimately requires us to directly face and deal with them in order to move on in a healthy way. It normally feels like hell while you are in the process of working through those events. My point above about drugs and religion is that both normally offer you an escape, and both can prevent you from processing through these events in a healthy way. Both keep you coming back to give you that "boost" you need, until that one wears off. Then you need to seek out the next "high". If one chooses to push these issues off during this life and not fully deal with them in this life, then hell could very well await you in the next life. You may have to deal with your issues there. I do not believe that passing from this life to the next will act like a magic eraser and eliminate all your problems. You may not have to return to your dead end job, but you may still need to deal with your hatred and bitterness. What a shock for the Christian expecting pearly gates and golden streets.

Modern Western Christianity teaches us that hell is something that happens to us in the afterlife if we do not subscribe to certain beliefs or doctrines. To believe in leaving this earth and magically ending up in the lap of the Father without worry or care seems a bit cheap to me. I believe hell can be experienced in the here and now or in the next reality. If one chooses to avoid it in this life, then it will still be waiting on you once you reach "the other side". I believe that many Christians used Christianity as a way of avoiding tough issues in this life with the promise of being whisked away to paradise upon their passing from this life. Heaven, a place of pure bliss, is marketed as a place one goes to after this life, where all of our worries and pain will magically disappear. There may or may not be this place of paradise after we pass on, however I do believe that we will need to deal with our problems before we pass into that paradise. There is also the possibility of sitting in the middle of that paradise, and the worries, anxiety, and pain of this life preventing one from enjoying it. It would be akin to believing that happiness will be attained with the purchase of the newest car or tech gadget. Once this "thing" is attained, there is a realization that the same problems still vex our souls. What I mean by this is that I do believe we are eternal beings. I believe there is infinite "life" available to us when we pass from this dimension. I however do not believe that this present experience or pain will just magically disappear. My personal belief is that whatever I do not fully process through and deal with in this life will need to be processed through in "eternity". Some things may only be fully recognized when one reaches eternity, where the layers of conditioning are stripped away, and everything can be seen clearly. I may not be able to see the full consequences of some of my actions until I reach the next dimension. This "vailed view" is in part why eternal damnation seems so unbecoming of eternal beings, and definitely unbecoming of an all-powerful god. I do not believe there will be a magical "whisking away" upon my passing away, into a place where all is suddenly well and where there is no sadness or grief. I believe there will be plenty for me to work through when I get there. I believe I will keep on being myself when I get there, wherever that may be. I believe that many Christians will be utterly shocked when they see who is actually seated at the "king's table", so to speak and will have a very hard time working through this conundrum.

I have had some Christians push back at me and say that they don't want Hitler or a child molester in heaven with them or their loved ones. I whole heartedly agree to that, but I don't believe that someone kneeling and saying a prayer to accept Jesus as his Lord and savior will magically make that person a non-child molester. Also, would you think it fair that a child that rejects Christianity because of the trauma that was caused from being abused deserves to be in hell right next to their abuser? Many pastors, priests, deacons, and so on have created many atheists, some did so through horrible acts of molestation and abuse. Do these abusers go to heaven because they prayed, and yet the atheist they crated goes to hell? Would true justice not be for the abuser to need to come to full grips with their evils, and for them to see full on the damage and pain they caused? Praying doesn't do that. I believe that the extraordinary amount of molestation and rape that goes on within the Christian community, among a vast amount of denominations, would attest to that. I don't believe that a prayer like that can just magically put away with the horrors of the Holocaust. Would the Jews who died in the Holocaust go to hell while Joseph Goebbels goes to heaven? In fact religion, Christianity in particular, was the fuel used by Joseph Goebbels (Hitler's propagandist) to drive and justify the horrors of the Holocaust. The Abrahamic religions in particular seem to be the most pliable religions of all and have been bent in such a way as to justify the most bloodthirsty events in history. It is actually very easy to do, and in some ways, the God of these religions kind of requires it. Normally religion is used as the glue that binds one group of people behind the horrific actions of nations that are intent on conquering another people group. Hitler could not have just pulled off the horrors of World War II if he would not have brought in a religious zealot as his propagandist. Christianity was used to rally, justify, and bind together the people behind Hitler's atrocities. This isn't a dig against Christianity, it's just the truth. So does Christianity save you from hell? No, it often creates it.

I have heard many times that God is a God of love and peace, but He is also a God of Justice. It is normally presented in such a way that God's love and mercy is subject to, or comes secondary to, his incessant need for justice. Normally a punishment of eternal hell is that justice. Escape from that justice is done through a simple prayer and an acceptance of Christ, without any real change needing to take place. There are many people and even whole people groups who have been severely damaged because of some heinous act of violence. When a perpetrator of a horrific crime was sentenced to death and executed, most of the people carrying the pain of these actions who were asked about this said that the execution of the perpetrator did little to nothing to satisfy their need for justice. It also did not heal their wounds. The pain was still there the same as it was before. In my experience, the only way that true justice can happen is if a perpetrator comes to the true realization of what they have done, and shows true repentance. If there is a utopian paradise, then I would hope that the pain dealers in this life would have to come to full grips with what we've done before we are allowed to enter. After all, I believe we can all admit that we have caused pain and heartache to someone in our lifetime. Where do we draw the line between severe heinous actions that REQUIRE justice, and hurtful actions that do not require justice? We would all like to think the pain we caused others was not that severe and is not in need of justice. Many of us have done things without knowing the true ripple effect of our actions. I highly doubt we know the full consequences of the pain we have caused. I sure hope there is copious amounts of grace there when I have to fully face the things I have done, and I hope whole heartedly that grace will lead into full justice. Only if one truly comes to full grips with something they have done can true justice take place. I don't believe that any prayer can deliver that realization, and the consequences of true atrocities may not be fully realized until you pass from this life. What if Hitler needs to make amends with 14 million people, as his heart aches, feeling the true pain that he has caused others? The ripple effects of his actions are still being felt today. What if he truly realizes that now? A person who has participated in violence and has seen the full consequences of these actions are the biggest advocates for peace. What if he, now as a truly humble soul, can now see the true effects of his decisions. Only when a soul has been humbled to that level can true repentance take place. I would actually say repentance would be inevitable. The pure and true intended nature of that person would then be realized. Such a person would then (in my opinion) be deserving of paradise, and paradise would be completely safe with that person in it. I would consider that true justice in its purest form.

I will say this as a side note about Christianity though. I do not believe that Christianity is anything close to what it was intended to be. I believe Christianity could hold way more power than what it currently does. I believe it is only a faint shadow of its origins. I am however neither a historian nor a scholar so my perception may be incorrect. If it is correct, then Christianity needs to go through a massive reformation that would far eclipse the days of Martin Luther and the protestant movement. In short, the protestant movement only rearranged and re-labeled the prover- bial furniture of the house and called it a new home. The current Western church still uses much of the same theology and damaging practices of the "pre-reformed" church and calls it a reformed or new church. If my perception is incorrect however, Christianity, rather than needing a drastic renovation may just need to be allowed to deteriorate or get burned away with the rest of our baggage, and used to fertilize the soil for something that offers a bit more hope to a world that is hurting so badly.

If humanity could agree that a truer, more pure sense of jus- tice is needed, then we could also restructure our prison systems, rehabilitation centers, etc…, to operate in a similar way as this. Our society could be fundamentally reshaped just by re-imagining what justice truly is. I don't have all the answers to how this would be done, but could we start moving in that direction? Would we be able to move from just locking up a "criminal" as punishment, to seeing a hurting individual and seek to lead that person to a true form of justice? Many so-called criminals are just locked up as punishment and no true effort is made to seek true change. Now mind you, I am talking of the prison systems in America. Criminals here are often released after a set amount of time without realizing anything and just end up being a repeat offender. They are given no new set of skills and no new hope for a better life. If we restructure our ideas of justice and what it truly is, then that more wholesome view of justice could seep into our society, effecting many other areas of life.

CHAPTER 14:

HEAVEN?

IF WE TALKED ABOUT HELL, then we definitely cannot leave out a conversation about heaven or its possibility. It turns out the talk of heaven is very similar to the talk of hell. The two are more similar than we give them credit, and at least the beginning of both can be realized in this life. The possibility of going to a blissful utopian paradise after this life certainly seems very attractive to most people. I mean who wouldn't want that right? Most view heaven as a place that you magically transport to, leaving all of your worries, cares, darkness, stress, hatred, and pain in this earthly existence. Is this how a view of heaven needs to be? Is this a healthy view of heaven? What are the benefits and drawbacks of this outlook? Do we all go there, or is it a privilege for a select few true believers? Of course to either prove or disprove any of these theories and perspectives is impossible. We choose to believe something the same way we choose our lifestyles. Some of this quite literally comes through a conscious choice, and some comes from the social conditioning we received in our lives. Either way, if you grew up in North America, you would probably have an outlook on heaven in a Western Christian way. Islam has its own perception of heaven or "paradise" as do other religions. Most religions have a slightly different view of what paradise is. You would also probably believe in heaven rather than reincarnation or a simple nonexistence if you were of a Western religion. In short, your view of heaven could almost be as much geographical as anything. What is the view of heaven based on? Most Christians do not realize that their whole eschatological outlook and beliefs boil down to just a few short passages in the bible. Most of these passages are collected throughout scripture and stitched together to form one big picture. One would be hard pressed to stitch together more than a few passages that would be considered good hard evidence of heaven, hell, and the existence of an afterlife at all. As mentioned in the previous chapter, if there is a heaven, then I believe it is attached to "hell", with the path to heaven going smack through the middle of "hell." All this means is that in order to experience paradise, one must come to true grips with all the pain and darkness of their being. This of course is a very painful process. That is what I mean by hell, not some fiery expanse that the eternally damned are thrown into.

So me personally, I like to believe in an afterlife. I still think there is some form of afterlife, but not necessarily the one handed down to me through tradition. For me, when I look around at everything, ranging from the microscopic organism to the expanse of the universe, I simply feel that there is more to me than what can be contained in this reality, on this earth, in a measly eighty something years of existence. I understand that a form of my previous religious self may be shining through in areas. I do however believe there is an inner knowing, an inner voice that screams out to this alternate reality beyond what is perceived here in the physical. The sense that some carry within themselves as being a divine creature is not just some silly notion because they don't want to die. I have heard it put this way and honestly, I believe it can be an oversimplified and flippant way of some people trying to ignore the possibility of an afterlife. With the view of an afterlife, there does come some semblance of an idea that wrongs, pain, anger, trauma, and overall hurtful actions will need to be dealt with in one form or the other. For some, the idea of an afterlife does not speak to them at all, and that is totally fine by me. I get it. As such, I am not stating dogmatically that there is life after death, because I am very well aware that it cannot be proven. I do not believe those who do not believe in life after death are silly in any way either. I just simply have something on the inside of me that seems to be telling me that there is. I feel this very strongly, and it's not because I am afraid of nonexistence. I understand the concept of nonexistence. I simply believe there is more. I believe we are sentient beings. I believe my spirit side of me is telling me this, because I believe I consist of more than my physical body. I believe there is the ability to perceive things in a way that does not make sense to the physical brain. Some would call this intuition. Where does intuition come from? Intuition can be a "knowing" of things that comes as almost more of a physical feeling at times. I believe that when I have an intuition that I can feel physically, it is a knowing or a memory that my spirit side of me is sharing with me physically. Sometimes these are so strong that my body may feel it in my "gut" or my physical brain may end up perceiving it as knowledge as well. Some people can even feel physical pain or ecstasy, depending on what their inner self is realizing. I do not know the ins and outs of evolution, but it is these things such as intuition, energies not seen, Ideas outside of ourselves, that to me, evolution itself cannot explain. (This, as a side note, is a concept that Christianity still holds on to very well in my opinion). I am not refuting evolution at all. I just think it needed help. I simply cannot view evolution as the single, all-powerful force that rules over the universe. Would this not also be believing in a form of all powerful god as well? If an evolutionary force drives this whole existence, then would evolution itself not be some form of god as well? To only claim belief in evolution is in my mind also claiming belief in a higher power that cannot be seen. Maybe my brain thinks a bit differently, but that is what it would seem like to me. I am not saying these things to be argumentative, but rather as an attempt to express my reasoning. I think evolution itself would have needed to be created the same as anything else. The very laws of the universe and unseen concepts around us would need a place of origin the same way a tree does. I think a tree and physical things around us can easily be explained through evolution, and I am happy for that. It is the unseen things that I believe are much harder to explain. Where does love come from? I have heard that love would have been an emotion developed through evolution, for survival the same as an arm or an opposing thumb would have evolved for survival. I am not knocking this idea because I am sure that makes sense to some people. I simply do not see it that way at all and my being simply seems unable to compute that ideology. It just seems way over simplified and cuts the true essence and power of love way too short. Once again, this may be due to my previous religious conditioning, but flippantly blowing it off (by me or someone else) as such would be doing an injustice to me as a person. I believe that for me it would just cheapen such a powerful force as love. It is these unseen realities, energies, laws, that seem to speak to my inner self, that testify to me that there is something beyond the grave, that I am a much bigger being than I could ever imagine. It seems to reveal that I am destined for something beyond my finite existence here, and arriving there may be more akin to waking up from this life rather than falling asleep in it.

Having a view of heaven as a place you go to that rescues you from this life has some very damaging consequences in my opinion. I believe the afterlife is heavily intertwined and influenced by this present existence. This belief of "rescue" can cause people to essentially ignore real problems in this life with the belief that if they survive to the end, all their troubles will go away. It also leads to being able to rape the planet because ultimately it will be destroyed anyway. Once one departs from this life, the belief is that it won't be their problem anymore. With the belief that death will solve all of your problems, people can ignore damaged relationships. People can ignore anxiety and depression. Hatred never needs to be dealt with if all pain and negative consequences will be washed away. Death almost becomes sought after as it is seen as the ultimate liberator, rescuing us from the struggles of this life. It leads people to either long for the future or a return to the past, but this view rarely compels one to live in the present. The past is usually glorified as better than the present with things only bound to get worse, until the ultimate end appears which will save us from all of this world's evils. These doctrines inherently have dark world views coursing through their veins. Some of these things may not even be conscious decisions or thoughts, however the implications are very clear and obvious. I think that humanity has lived long enough under these pretenses that it is almost a part of our DNA at this point. I think these systems and world views have had such power for so long that these outlooks have permeated society beyond what we even realize. The cognitive dissonance is almost bred into the theology with decisions being made even subconsciously, and dark outlooks on humanity and creation being passed down generationally. One could be completely atheistic, claiming no spirituality whatsoever, and yet make decisions based on religion due to the fact that religions were used as the foundational blocks for our society for so long. Religion courses through civilization and its systems because religion was used to create them. We have had doctrines and theology painting a very dark tunnel for humanity, where the present existence is something to only be endured, with the light at the end of the tunnel being death. This leads to inaction by many people in the present world, while they pray for Jesus to return quickly. Many believe they are powerless to enact change, so the fight is lost before the first punch is even thrown. The church building has become a modern Noah's Ark where one can run to in order to ride out the storm. No wonder we have a hard time being present in the here and now. How depressing.

Me personally I like the idea of a "heaven", but I do not necessarily believe in a "Christian" view of it. Like I mentioned previously, the Christian view of heaven does not seem that desirable to everyone. I believe this again is a place where our creative imagination can be used. I wouldn't let any teachings from churches and spiritual leaders step in the way here, because as I mentioned there is absolutely no way of stitching together a solid view of heaven from biblical passages. Believing that we are eternal beings, we must conclude that something exists after this life. If we choose another realm of existence outside of this one, then it seems logical to me that it would be heavily influenced by my experiences here on this earth. If I will be influenced "there" by what happens "here" then I would also believe I would hold on to my personality. I would hang on to what makes Steve, Steve. I would also think that all the emotional experiences here of love, joy, hatred, and pain would also shape my experiences there. Maybe the pain I experience here could help me strive for and enjoy a time without pain. Maybe this realm is where I learn to love. Maybe the hatred and anger that I experience here will help me further appreciate the love I experience there. Sadness here could give me a solid measuring device for joy there. If I did not experience sadness here, would I really know what joy was there? If I had no baseline to measure from, would joy and love just seem normal and "meh" or would it even exist there? There may be something so wonderful that is available in the next realm of existence, that we are willing to go through this existence in order to get to it. Maybe there is something so important about this existence that we are willing to leave paradise to come here for a while. Some believe that we chose to come here. If we are eternal beings, then we would need to exist in the past as well. Maybe I chose my reality here much the way a gamer chooses an avatar, world, and difficulty level when playing a game. Maybe I knew what would serve me best in eternity and I chose this life for that reason. Maybe my loved ones are the ones I chose to exist with because they really are the best ones for me, and will impact me forever. I may have seen something so desirable here that I put on this skin, said "I'll be back in a bit", and dove in headfirst. Who knows? Maybe I saw what my fellow beings were doing here on this earth, and I decided I wanted to be part of it. Maybe I saw that I could help move things forward just a bit.

I also do not believe that all the dark things attached to me here will magically fall away from me during my transition into the next existence. Sure, maybe I will have the chance to see loved ones again, so the loneliness of their absence would disappear. The pain of losing them and how that experience shaped your life would probably not magically disappear. That would essentially be undoing the experiential knowledge of that event, rendering it meaningless. The things we experience here must follow us there, or what would these experiences accomplish? Also, if I harbor great hatred and malice towards anyone or anything in this life, then I will need to face those same emotions there. Maybe a "vail" of sorts will be lifted from my eyes and I can perceive things more clearly, but I believe that clarity would only be there to help me better work through my pain. If the universe were open to me and yet I could not enjoy it due to my lingering anxiety, it would cause me to deal with it in very short order. I don't mean that things would be deliberately withheld from someone, but more in the way that you cannot fully appreciate the taste of your favorite food if you are full of anxiety. In this way, I would believe that a form of "hell" awaits all of us at the entrance to paradise. I believe to the "righteous" crowd, coming to the realization that all pain and anxiety did not magically disappear may be particularly painful. It may be particularly painful for some when they see who all is there enjoying themselves and having a ripe good time.

What about the place? Is there a city made of gold? Maybe, if that's what you need it to be. I believe the "universe" or "god" can be whatever you need it to be at the time that you need it. If you are a Christian and would be absolutely wrecked if you couldn't live inside a city with golden streets, then you could probably have it. As for me, I'll be busy exploring other things such as the distant reaches of the solar system, or maybe I'll get to experience the mountains, desserts, beaches, and plains of this earth. Maybe I will have the chance to experience this earth in a way I never could while I was "alive". Maybe this life is more like being dead, and I will become alive on the other side of existence. Maybe my vision of paradise is to chill with all of my loved ones around a giant bonfire. Maybe all of this is possible whenever you desire it. If you begin your "eternity journey" inside the pearly gates and you begin to wonder what is outside of those gates, you may just be able to go do it. If a loved one desires to be surrounded by family, and yet you wish to be sitting on Mars watching the stars go by, both could be possible simultaneously. Who says that space and time need to be obstacles? Why can heaven or paradise not be whatever you desire it to be? If it would shatter a poor soul to reach the "other side" and not be greeted by their contemporary view of heaven, Saint Peter at the pearly gates and all, then I believe they could have that. Maybe it would be there to greet them, but their vision of it may need to expand over time as their realization increases. Once again, it can be what a person NEEDS at the time as well. I do believe in order for one to fully enjoy paradise, they must first deal with the things they have experienced here. If this existence does not affect one's existence there then what's the point? I will still be Steve when I get there, however I may just not have the limitations of this realm anymore. I would like to believe that I could build my own creature companion. Something with a dragon's neck and head, with the body of Pegasus, but being black in color with bright red wingtips. If there is a God I could go show it off to him/her. We would all look at it and admire it. I'd name it my "Majestic Whatthefuck". We'd all get a good chuckle. We'd pass the bong one more time, then for a thousand years, or until I've had enough, I'd jump on my magical steed and go explore places I always wanted to see, ride to far reaching galaxies in search of interesting planets and do anything I wanted to do. I mean seriously, lets make this interesting. Maybe you don't want to hit a bong with god, but maybe I do. I don't want to sit around paying homage to some narcissistic deity for eternity. I do not want to be trapped inside city walls regardless how nice they are. A nonexistent eternity would almost sound more appealing to me than a traditional view of heaven.

CHAPTER 15:

_____

WHAT ABOUT EVIL?

"Man cannot remake himself without suffering, for
he is both the marble and the sculptor."

~Alexis Carrell~ 1873-1944

WHAT ABOUT EVIL THEN? THIS is the big question we all seem to ask, "How does this explain evil?" I don't think anyone has an explanation of evil that works for everyone, and neither do I. I have some ideas that make sense to me... kind of. It helps me, and seems to be the best I can do. As for you? Just like the rest of this book, you can choose to hang on to it and use it, or you can throw it in the trash when you're done reading it.

To put it simply, evil is something that we do. It is something we bring into this world. If we are creators as I have expressed before, we are capable of creating evil. If one is capable of magnificent goodness, the opposite is true as well. With the universe being a direct reflection of divinity and us, every action also has an equal and opposite reaction. Evil could be described as the absence of good or love, the same way darkness is just the absence of light, and cold is just the absence of heat. If something happens within us that detaches us from good, we would act in a not so kind way in direct correlation to the extent that you have been severed from good. An object will get cold to the degree that it is removed from heat. Do you want to change a person that has done some very dark things? Don't focus on the bad they have done, but rather get them in touch with the good that is inside them. Do not simply punish them for the bad they have done, but make them aware of the goodness they are capable of. The same way we cannot create absolute zero, a person is never completely devoid of goodness.

Believing that nature is mimetic of us and our current state, I also believe much of the sickness and disease are a direct reflection of how well we are doing as a species. Keeping an eye on how tumultuous creation is would be akin to monitoring one's heartbeat or blood pressure. A mosquito is not an evil insect, yet it has killed more people than any other animal. This poor thing has only been used as an attachment for malaria and other diseases. You could say that the mosquito is almost as much a victim of malaria as the person that it kills. To call the mosquito evil because it is capable of carrying malaria could be a little short sighted.

For most of my life I was taught that at the core of my being lies all that is corrupt and evil, you know, because of the fall and all that stuff. Most people believe that their default is evil, and goodness is something to be gained or achieved. Coming from the religious world, we are taught that we need to have a covering for this evil, whether it is a white robe, or the covering of the blood of Jesus. In short, we need something to cover and obscure the evil within us. This is akin to someone placing a napkin over a dog turd on the kitchen floor until their partner comes home to dispose of it. You would still know it's there, you can still smell it, it'll bother you the whole time, but at least you don't have to see it. I have found that the thing that actually brought real healing and change into my life was realizing the opposite is true. I had goodness inside of me. I was born with it. Life and bad circumstances placed layers and layers over this goodness. I had a lot of love and kindness in me. They were just really hard to see sometimes through all the layers that had been placed over them. In other words, I was a clean house with clean floors, then people, bad circumstances, religion, etc… were like the dogs that came and shit all over my floors. I know this isn't the best analogy, but it's what I got, alright? I was attempting to place napkins over all this shit in my life, believing this is what I had to do until God came back to make me clean again. God never came to clean it up and my house became disgusting. I had to realize it was time for me to take matters into my own hands and throw this shit out. To make matters worse, some of the very things taking a huge dump in my life were some of the very things giving me the napkins to place over the turds. Christianity, by teaching me I was evil and defiled was much like an evil doctor in a movie, giving you poison to make you sick in order to sell you the medicine to make you better. The only problem is you will always be fed poison and the medicine is always snake oil. They are guaranteed to have a return customer if they never fully let you get better. It seems that to get better, some of us just need to stop ingesting the poison. I once again want to be careful here. I am criticizing the system, not the people caught up in it. Sure some are deliberate perpetrators, but most are well intentioned people who are just as much a victim of the system as anyone else is. Having such a dark outlook on one's self and humanity plays right in to what I described previously in the book. This outlook causes people to sit still in the face of all that is wrong in this world, believing and waiting for a divine savior to come clean it all up. Much of the Christian world does not believe we can achieve things such as world peace because their theology teaches them things will perpetually get worse until their savior comes back. This takes us back to the "fight being over before the first punch is even thrown" or the poison and snake oil analogy.

It is my belief that the divine power that is needed to fix this place and this society lies within us. This power IS us. You don't just have this power, you ARE this power. It is almost as if society is coming in to this realization, and yet the current world systems are holding us back. Governments, religions, and even large corporations could potentially have a lot to gain by keeping things the same. We have a fairly large movement in the good ole USA that keeps wanting us to return to the past, to "the good ole days." Unfortunately the good ole days always seems to be the American 1950's. This movement has this idealistic image in its head of strong conservative values, and little Johnny and little Sue sitting around the dinner table with their parents. This however is an unrealistic idea of the era and overlooks the absolute horrors going on at the time. Many of the horrors were actually created by this very system that they want to take us back to. The 40's, 50's, 60's, and 70's were a cesspool of violence and death of all kinds. We had some of the most deadly wars in history. Racism was at its peak and the world was at the verge of nuclear holocaust. These decades have been some of the most deadly ones ever, and they lay within the deadliest century in human history. We humans created this evil and we should not cast blame on some detached devil. I want anything but the American "good ole" days. We all should.

Back in my evangelical days, talk of revival was almost an occurrence every Sunday. Even as an evangelical I got sick and tired of hearing the word. I grew to dislike it, because I saw it as a tool that essentially dangled a carrot in front of the congregation's nose and kept them coming back for more. I remember telling people that if revival does come, the church won't know it even if it bit them in the face. I said that this one wouldn't look like any other one. The pastors were so focused on a new Billy Graham, Benny Hinn, Charles Spurgeon type of revival with people splayed out at the alter and some pastor huffing and puffing into a microphone. These revivals were always more internally focused, with current Christians coming in to refuel more than anything else. Sure there were some new converts, but in reality, they just rallied up the current believers more than anything and did not influence outsiders as much as one would think. I remember telling people that if a revival really is coming it won't be happening inside the church buildings. We need something that feeds all of humanity, not just Christianity. If you limit an enlightening to being inside churches or in tent meetings, and only in a Christian context then you have already limited how many can participate. Maybe church leaders from all different religions need to take the blinders off and take a look at the current shift that is happening now. This movement is not happening inside church walls and is not led by the older generation. This movement is happening in the hearts of the common folks, and our young ones are leading the way. The "revival" is trying to take place, but it looks way different than expected. It looks so different that it isn't even recognized by many. This "revival" is being inhibited by the ones who don't like what it looks like.

In reality, if the younger generation is wanting things to change then they have to be the ones to lead it, because our older generation is too busy criticizing them for being different. The younger generation is usually criticized for not wanting to work. This is such a lie. They simply see the idiocrasy of wasting one's life away in a nine to five job. Retirements are getting harder and harder to attain. Both partners need full time careers. In reality a nine to five isn't enough anymore. The amount of time spent earning a living is increasing, and retirement seems to be slipping away for most. The younger generation is required to work longer and harder for less pay and benefits keep being taken away. The cost of healthcare and education keep increasing by leaps and bounds. They find themselves in a place where they become poorer while working to make corporations wealthier. The reality is that this younger generation is some of the most passionate people I have seen on the planet. Place something they are passionate about in front of them and they will pursue it with all they have. They are hungry for change! Their passions are simply different than those of the past. The newer generations are more passionate about things that propel humanity forward. They want to reinvigorate the science community. They want to go back to space. They want to make humanity better! Prior generations were stifled, and my generation along with some older ones, just fell into the normal way things are done without giving it much question. We have conformed to systems rather than challenging them. To be fair, some of us found ourselves caught up in a post 9/11 world where we came of age fighting the longest war in American history, coupled with one of the worst economic recessions in our history. Many people in their 30's to people in their 50's were too busy trying to survive. We didn't have much energy left to "rage against the machine." I feel as though my generation (30's – 40's) is kind of caught in the middle trying to choose between two ideologies. The older generation is trying to pull the younger generations back into their way of doing things, into their way of seeing things. I am not hating on our parent's generation. Many of them did the best they could with what they could. Even though there were problems there, our parent's generation also fought to desegregate society and there was also a big "peace" movement in their day. The previous generations did not fail, but we also need to be allowed to move forward. I think that a great movement was started back in their day and was largely overlooked, and even stifled. It seems now that the generation that was to a degree shut down and stifled, may be trying to do the same to this current generation. This current younger generation, even younger than I, sees something. They are tired of the same old thing. They don't like seeing the world stagnant and in turmoil. I am proud of our young ones. They decided they want to see change and they are out creating it. Don't stop them. Go out and support them! If you think that the younger generation seems lost, it may be due to them needing to blaze their own trail without the support of their elders. Any generation would struggle to find themselves if all they hear is criticism coming from their supposed mentors.

Change is always difficult, and our establishments have spent many years opposing it. Change is necessary. I believe this is why our reality is so tumultuous right now. There is a large portion of society that has evolved beyond what our current systems can handle. Some have been hooked by current systems and are trying to pull us back. Change is inevitable, but sometimes the ones trying to advance simply need to give it time until their numbers become so large and their movement gains so much momentum that change becomes inevitable. If we want society to calm down, if we want the planet to rest, if we want creation to smile, then we must continue to progress. We must allow ourselves to evolve. To not allow change is like cutting off the flow of water to a body of fresh water. It will progressively become more and more stagnant until it becomes a toxic cesspool, until it becomes poison to anyone who drinks from it. Water must continue to flow in order to stay healthy. The same is true for humanity. There is absolutely nothing bad or wrong with change. We must become friends with it on both a personal and societal level.

I say all of this to portray a picture of a society that is attempting to change things for the good. I am attempting to portray a society that is aware of the power that it holds. It sees the evil and damage of the past, and desires to move into a better tomorrow. I do not want to degrade or devalue the innocence and of a whole past generation. Of course there were great people. Of course they had great times. Of course those memories of the past are to be cherished. Of course the memory of childhood was just as innocent then as it is now. But these individual memories should not be used as a tool to overlook the atrocities that the systems around them forced onto other people. These systems of the past, likewise, should not be used to project evil onto the individual of the past. To undo the wrongs of society, however, society must be allowed to move away from the past. A realization of the injustices of the past is not an unhealthy thing. If we created the evils of this world, and we are aware of that, we can also undo these evils. We can create a different world. We can quite literally create whatever world that we envision.

CHAPTER 16:

CREATORS

SO WHO ARE WE? WHY are we here? Am I just a bag of bones without much power or purpose? Am I only here to be rescued by death? Am I just a "fallen creature in a fallen world?" Do we just need to suffer this world and merely exist in a messed up reality that us humans have created? Do we have the power to change this world? Would we not, in general, regardless of religious preference, agree that the mess we see around us is something that we as humans have created? Christianity or most other religions don't want to blame their god, atheists don't believe in a god, so the only thing left is us, right? So we created this. The debates could rage on and on about how we progressed to this point and what the forces are behind it all. If we can all agree on the point that we as humans have created this mess, then that is one small step forward. We could then agree that we can, at least a little, have the power to create the reality around us. If we can create evil, we should also be able to create good in a likewise manner. We create nations and the wars they fight. We created our economic systems. We create good things as well such as modern medicine and state of the art care facilities. We create rockets that take us out of earth's atmosphere. We created airplanes that enable us to see other places and cultures as never before. We can also use rockets and airplanes to blow each other up. We have all of these things that we have created, and we have the ability to decide how we will use them. Economic systems can also be used in much the same way. Even a good economic system can be used to destroy other economies, from local competition, to other national economies. We decide how we use the tremendous things that we have created. Our use of these things has created the reality around us. If we do not like the condition of the world we live in, we have the ability to change it. We can create something new.

I believe that we have the ability to create anything we want. I quite literally believe that our ability to create is only limited by our imagination, or more specifically, by how far we will allow ourselves to imagine. I think that we limit our imaginative power in direct correlation to how vulnerable we are willing to be. I believe quantum mechanics is already making discoveries leading to some of this. The great minds that are exploring this quantum realm are leaning that at least part of our universe does not operate in a logical way, or in ways that we see our physical world around us. They are making discoveries of tiny particles that only manifest when they are observed. Some particles are more of a wave, not really being anywhere, but yet at the same time, having the possibility of being anywhere, just waiting to be observed. It's almost as if these particles and energies are making themselves available to anyone, anywhere, at any time. They are just waiting for someone to give them space, or permission to exist through the realization their possibilities. By realizing and recognizing their possibility, they then manifest as real particles. Some of these particles seem to be connected to each other, being able to communicate and effect the other particle instantaneously. It is as if space and time does not exist between these particles. Could the attributes of the quantum level somehow be brought into our realm of existence? Are there energies and capabilities out there, floating around, with the possibility of being pulled into reality? Is the only thing separating us from an unimaginable existence, our willingness to imagine, to give space to things that sound impossible to us now? Are there possibilities or laws of the universe, that just need permission to exist? What if I (or you or anyone), emitting energy waves and frequencies as unseen potentials of myself, could have the possibility of being anywhere, instantaneously? Could we humans be interconnected in a way that quantum particles are, with the ability to communicate amongst each other, with no regard of space and time? The crazy thing is that physicists and such, use these "theories" already in our communications systems, computers, and nuclear energy programs. It really does work on the quantum level. Maybe none of this is possible on our larger level, however I do believe it deserves exploration especially since there are elements of existence that do seem to work this way. Some of these elements already interact with us in these ways. To go outside the box of thought and imagination requires vulnerability with ourselves and others. Sometimes it seems as though we are afraid of imagining too much. Maybe we are afraid of what others will think if they would only know our wildest imaginations. Our imagination is just as much a strength of ours as the muscles in our arms. You as a person can have all the athletic capabilities in the world, but you will not achieve anything with those capabilities if you cannot first imagine yourself achieving something. I graduated basic training not because I was faster, stronger, or better than those that failed, but because I could imagine myself doing it. I believed that it was something I could achieve, and I did. Landing humans on the moon would still be impossible, and would remain so forever if it had not been imagined first. They believed they I could, so they did. Our ability to do anything is more a battle of the imagination than it is of actual capability. I quite simply cannot do much of anything if I cannot imagine myself doing it. Some may call this having vision and goals. I believe our imagination or vision can quite literally create all possibilities. It is almost as if imagination can pull things from another dimension, into our dimensional realm so that we can bring it into reality. I think it goes beyond the analogy of something simple like not being able to build a cedar chest until you imagine it. I believe it literally pulls unrealistic things into our realm of existence. It manifests it in an almost spiritual way. It is the bridge on which things from a foreign realm travel into our realm. If we want something such as world peace or a world without disease, we must first imagine it and dare to believe it is possible. I believe that this is where traditional prayer and faith fail. We normally pray to a god that is somewhere out "there" somewhere and ask him/her to come intervene, change, or create something. We focus our imaginative power on an abstract god, and not on that which we want to change. It is as if we were to intentionally aim at a different target than the one we wish to hit, in hopes that the projectile will ricochet and hit the real target. Our energies come from within us and can be aimed or focused on our targets themselves. To focus your energy on a god to enact the change for you is like randomly blasting out into space, sending your energies to a place where they accomplish little to nothing. You have the power to change things. Focus your energies on the change you wish to happen, and then do it. You ARE the power that is needed in this world. There is no need to go to an outside source. I believe that our capabilities are limitless. We must imagine a way of existence that has never been attempted before. We must imagine possibilities that have never been dreamt of before. It will take beings from all around the planet, from all different lifestyles to do this. It must be a collective imagination. Normally imagination will not actually bring the possibility into tangibility. That takes action, but action without vision is pointless.

So what if we as a collective body of spirits can actually create possibilities? One person's focused energy is powerful, but what if it were a bunch of focused energies from around the planet? How powerful could that be? Take for instance the theory of quantum entanglement. What if through time, starting from early civilization, there were a collective energy that was placed in or towards ideas, ultimately ending up with great minds such as Einstein, Bohm, John Bell, etc... Now even though Einstein refuted quantum entanglement, the paper he co-authored drew immense attention to the idea. This led to many great minds focusing energy towards the idea. As time progressed to today, we are discovering very quickly that this theory proves more and more true as time goes on. Sure things are modified, added to, or subtracted from as more things are discovered, but these discoveries would not be possible if the concepts were not first imagined. Energies needed to be focused, and then pursued. So, maybe, just maybe the collective mind of many beings that is focused on a single point like a laser beam can actually take an idea or theory, and create a possibility. The imagination of people can project possibilities out in front of humanity that enables us to walk in to them. It would be like an advanced party of individuals building bridges across rivers so that the rest of their convoy can just walk across them. Through the exploration of possibilities, coupled with focused action, can turn that possibility into reality. This is way over simplified from what I want to convey. What if the imagination of a unified existence without war, famine, and disease is attainable? What if not having to waste your life away at a dead end job in order to attain material possessions is possible? What if the idea of "possession" doesn't need to be a thing? What if communication and travel over vast distances could be possible without phone or vehicle? So, what if the theory that two particles, one here on earth and the other in another galaxy can somehow be connected, or the theory that space technically does not exist, could somehow lead to the possibility of instant and effortless transportation? What if "teleporting" to anywhere you wish would become as common as jumping on an airplane and flying to the next city? Maybe it could lead to the eradication of disease, or make the healing of disease possible without the use of medicine. Maybe healing through the transfer or focus of energy is possible. It may just not need to be routed or ricocheted off of a deity first. Maybe this journey transcends the personal journey and is more of a collective journey with endless possibility. It's just an idea.

What about the idea of possession? This endless rat race we run in in order to possess a TV, truck, cell phone, etc…, may not be necessary. I may not know how it all would work out, but the existence of such monotony could be eliminated. The idea of our need to possess something largely comes from an idea of lack, or the need for power and stature. The idea that there isn't enough to go around is a false belief in my opinion, especially when it comes to the necessities. The idea of possession is used by nations to gain wealth and power. They think that in order to have you must go get something and keep it for yourself. The idea that there isn't enough to go around will cause people to go out and attain for themselves without the thought of other's needs. We store up food in pantries or bug out shelters while others starve to death. My ability to have food in abundance is not wrong, but everyone should have enough to eat. It is not the ability to enjoy nice things that is the problem. The problem is when a portion of society is prospering while others are barely surviving. When the European's came over and signed treaties with the natives for land, many natives did not know in full what they were signing. The native's had almost no concept of personal land ownership. It could maybe be considered more accurately as resource ownership. The land and everything on it was a resource to be shared among each other. I do not believe they viewed land and resources as something that could even be possessed by humans. It was all communal land. They were a part of the land the same as any other creature. They all enjoyed it equally and together. There may have been tribal territories, but hard physical possession was not really a thing. Their idea of allowing Europeans onto the land was either thought of as a temporary thing, or welcoming Europeans to come share the land with them. They had no intention of Europeans possessing the land for themselves, and definitely did not want to forfeit the use of it. This does not mean they did not have any personal possessions such as clothing or similar things, but personal resource possession was largely a foreign concept. This idea of communal access to resources does not strip away your access to things, but can actually open up greater access to more things.

As a side note, I am not talking about some government legislated programs. I know right where many people will go with this, and I want to stop it here. It has to be a socially adopted thing and not a governmentally legislated thing. I may elaborate on this later. Once again, I think this must be imagined as something outside of what societies know today. I am not talking about simply changing to a socialist economy. Think of communities sharing amongst each other freely and willingly.

If we created our world around us, have we also created disease and famine? What about the tumultuous weather patterns we see? Did we create cancer, polio, malaria, scoliosis, and the like? Did we create tornadoes, global warming, and tsunamis? If we didn't create some of these things, are they within our power to tame, much like taming a wild beast? Maybe weather has always been harsh, but maybe we can conquer its peaks much the same as we conquered Everest. Maybe these things are mimetic, painting a clear picture of the human condition? I do look at nature entirely differently than I used to. I look at the things such as trees, snow, Ice, grass, and things without breath in their lungs as something that is alive. I now look at them as something that can feel, and if it cannot understand my physical voice, it can understand me as a being and understand my outlook of it. I find myself talking to things such as trees and even apologizing for things I do. This may sound crazy, but give me a minute. Haha! I was walking this morning through the remnants of an ice storm that moved in last night. The tree branches are all beautifully encased in about a quarter inch of ice, with tiny icicles hanging everywhere. Even though there was no sunshine, everything was sparkling and pretty. I decided to take a walk through the back field on a trail that skirts some trees. As I was walking I enjoyed how pretty it all was, but eventually got lost in thought. I inadvertently smacked an ice encased tree branch to knock the ice off of it. As soon as I did that I wondered why I would do that? Why would I hit something so pretty just to damage it and break apart the very beauty I came to see? I wondered why I needed to do those things, and why I couldn't enjoy nature for what it is and not feel the need to tamper with it? If I see a pretty flower, why can I not admire its beauty and then leave it there to flourish? Why do we pick something like that, just to have it die in a vase on our dining room table? As crazy as it sounds, I went back to the tree and apologized for hitting it. I felt as though nature came together and dressed itself up in pretty clothing to catch the admiration of anything willing to notice, and here I went and smacked it. I felt bad. I felt as though I insulted that tree. I know this may sound silly, but I did. When I apologized I actually felt as though I was apologizing to a person. I felt as though I connected. I felt as though that tree understood. Even if the tree/creation did not understand, it still did something inside me, that benefitted my inner self. There have even been studies to show this true, with plants flourishing greatly when positive energy and words were directed at them. The same plant right next to the flourishing plan would wither and look sickly when negative words and energy were directed at it. Ever wonder why a person can seem to have a "green thumb"? you will often find these people talking and singing to their plants. They genuinely love the plants they tend. Even if one would argue that it is silly to think a tree can understand a person, the benefit goes beyond the tree. The benefit can be personal, and it can reach the heart. It will cause a person to connect with something even if it is only within one's self. When you connect with something, it causes you to respect it for what it is. It enables you to give it the space it deserves in this existence. Without trees and such, we could not be here. Connection limits the abuse and flippant nonrecognition of things. If we could talk to and treat creation as a living and conscious thing, even if you do not believe that it is, it will at least create a respect for it that could at the least cause us to look at it as more than a resource to be attained and pillaged. Nature feeds us physically and spiritually. Nature is food for the soul. Anyone who has spent time out in nature, and anyone that has truly experienced it can attest to the fact that it is a place where peace can be found. A reconnection to one's self can be found there as if a part of us is roaming about in nature, waiting for us to discover it. The reconnection to ourselves can come through connection with nature. The things of nature around us belong here and have a right to this place as much as us. Without us, nature would flourish. Without nature, we die. Sometimes I feel as though nature adorns itself in beauty, just hoping it will be recognized and admired, much like a person wanting recognition from their partner. I think if we could get ourselves to view nature in this way, we would be much kinder and more gentle to it.

With some studies that have shown plants struggling to survive when spoken to harshly, and others thriving greatly when spoken to kindly, it would appear as though nature can be mimetic, at least to a degree. It is said that the singing of song birds in the mornings helps plants to grow more bountifully. I do not have the information to this study, but it sure would show the interconnectedness of it all. I believe this is only the beginning of the discovery of our connectedness with nature, and the universe in general. If plants can pick up on our energy and react accordingly, could weather and disease do the same? Maybe climate change goes beyond just greenhouse gasses. Sure, abundant greenhouse gasses could affect this, and could also serve as a sign of our neglect of the planet, but could it go deeper? Could new diseases and the increase of things such as heart problems be just as much, if not more, a product of the internal human condition as it is the things we eat? Could the energy we cast out from us be absorbed by the planet and be released as hurricanes and tornadoes? Could the bitterness within us be somehow perceived by nature, mimicking it back to us the way a child mimics a parent? Could the bitterness and hatred in our hearts be turned into cancer and heart disease? Where do new diseases come from? Aside from conspiracy theories, could the black plague, the Spanish flu, and Covid be a reflection of society's condition at any given time? Rather than a lab in Wuhan, could all of humanity and our violence, in a collective way, have been the petri dish of these viruses? If we can create the nasty things that plague us through the energies we cast out from us, could we also bring healing by doing the opposite? I believe we can. I think if we got our shit together and began living harmoniously, both with other humans as well as with nature, our positive energies will be absorbed by creation and reflect it back to us. Why not? We quite literally have nothing to lose by trying it. If nothing else it will positively impact you as a person. It will penetrate your heart and change you. Do not waive it off as silly until the possibility has at least been explored. Consider it a new frontier of exploration.

If sickness, disease, and famine are a reflection of the human condition, could the evil in this world be a similar reflection? I feel as though much of the evil we experience is a product or creation of our own systems. The societal systems and structures that we have created is causing humanity to live as something other than our true selves. Religion has taught people that they are inherently bad, evil, and corrupt creatures. Nations and economic systems have caused people to waste their lives away at dead end jobs, and cause us to prop up governments that only seek power and riches. Governments create nationalism which leads to wars and exploitation. If we teach humanity that we are inherently evil and then create systems to further oppress them, then of course there will be violence and all sorts of evil running about. What the hell do we expect? We are quite literally writing our own horror film and then wondering why everything sucks so bad. We can rewrite this film into something much better and brighter. If we quit shadow boxing with evil powers, demons, and devils then maybe we would have the energy and focus to pursue something better. Remember, you have the possibility of giving life to what you focus on. If you focus on demonic possessions, then you will create the very demons that you fight. You have the ability to manifest your own demons, the same way that you can manifest your own tranquility. If the devil is behind every bush, your world will be full of fear and darkness. If the devil is nothing to be concerned about, then you can live in joy and happiness. If you imagine something as being impossible, then it will always remain impossible to you. If you view humanity and this creation as something glorious, you can live within that existence. The world can quite literally be what you make of it, but you have to start while everything around you is in chaos.

CHAPTER 17:

HOW DO WE END THIS?

THIS WHOLE THING, THIS EXISTENCE, this time, this space, this book, is all, in a roundabout way, all about you. It all comes down to the personal and individual level. This is where this all should end. You, yourself, nothing else, are the most powerful thing that can bring about any amount of change that you would like to see. Implement the change within yourself, then focus your energy on living it out. Envision a future that you would like to live in. Create a path, build a bridge for others to walk on. Focus your energy on being happy. Let that positive energy radiate out into everything around you. Creation, the universe will absorb that energy, and act in kind. The quickest way to bring about positive change is to bring it about in yourself. Inevitably, focusing positive energy on yourself will always spill out on your surroundings.

We find mirroring, on the physical and spiritual levels to be offensive. Why? Because it reflects an element of ourselves that is either actively present, or it reveals a belief we hold of ourselves on a subconscious level. Just like looking into a mirror in the bathroom in the morning, when someone mirrors our own actions, beliefs about ourselves, personality traits, etc., we often pick up/focus on the flaws that are revealed. We normally do not see this as mirroring or realize what is happening, because it is much easier to pass off the offender to just being a jerk, or to vilify anything that hurts us emotionally. Maybe we just end up not being friends with someone because we are just not "compatible". Maybe it would be healthy to ask if we cannot be comfortable around that person, not because there is something wrong with them, but because they are mirroring something back to us that we do not like about ourselves. If we become vehemently opposed to or offended by a statement or action by any other entity other than ourselves, it is often reflecting back to us an image we carry of ourselves. This can range from a micro personal level, all the way up to a macro national level. A person such as myself, may have huge issues with a parent. Sure there may be real pain to heal from, but sometimes it is more a case of seeing elements of the very actions that hurt me, within myself. If a parent verbally or physically abused you (or whatever it may be), you definitely need the space to heal and feel your emotions about those offenses, however sometimes we also need to check and make sure that some of the pain isn't coming from seeing some of the same traits within ourselves. A person will often become offended by a spouse, not because they do something wrong, but because they reveal a deep seated belief about one's self. A "conservative" will often become so enraged at "liberal" policies and politicians, in part, because there is an element or capability of themselves that they see in that "liberal" policy or politician. Sometimes it may be because we see the opposing party fighting against (or promoting) a so-called evil that we see in ourselves. The same is true in reverse of course. We see a side of ourselves that scares us. We see a side of ourselves that we have been raised to believe is wrong. Homophobic much? Maybe there is an element of yourself that you see there? Maybe your religion has taught you this is something evil or something to be afraid of. Maybe your religion has taught you this is a sure ticket to hell. This conditioning is all fear based, and will cause you to kick back violently at the element of it that you see within yourself, manifesting itself as being homophobic. We Americans are so enraged and offended by Russian aggression in Ukraine, not because it is something new, but because it is a mirror reflection of what America has been doing for a long time now. Our government is criticizing Russia's actions so intently because it is afraid the world will see the same evils within it as well. It often serves well to pay attention to what offends you. You will often find that it reveals either a characteristic or a belief of one's self that needs some attention. It often reveals areas that require healing.

Most of the time it is much easier to attempt to hire out the change and advancement that we wish to see in society to a third party. We do this all the time, and almost everyone has done it. We often hope that electing the right government official, donating to the local shelter, tithing to the right church, etc., with similar viewpoints as us, will somehow affect the change that we wish to see in society. It is much easier to donate food to the local shelter than it is to see an element of yourself in the homeless person on the corner. Once I see myself in that person, maybe it will cause me to BE the change that I want to see. That is hard to do though, and becomes very uncomfortable. Once I saw myself as a middle eastern man attempting to live a good life with my family, it forced me to see "him" as myself. Maybe he/she is only interested in what the James Webb Space Telescope will discover, or the next advancement in medicine, but a tank sits outside their home, and their family was ripped apart by warring governments. Once I saw the struggling Iraqi family as my precious little family, it changed everything. As such, it made me second guess my position on war, and the privilege I have as an American. There is no good vs evil in war. The people paying the price are never the ones who created the evils that led to the war. Once I realized that government systems did not have this same capability, to look into the interconnectedness of humanity, it forced me to view politics in a different way. A political party is a governmental system, without feelings, without connectedness. It contains absolutely nothing that makes us human. A system will always do what it was created to do, and will do so without emotion, but relies on our participation to remain alive. These systems are essentially entities that we have created, gave them life, then became detached from us, and now require our energy to keep them alive. This is very much how the dark/evil/demonic (whatever you call it) realm exists as well. Evil is something we created, we gave it life, and it requires our focused energy to sustain itself. If you are still in the Christian realm of things, please go check out a podcast where Brad Jersak and Michael Hardin toss around the idea of "the Satan". The podcast is "Beyond The Box" and the episode title is "The Satan". Even though it is coming from a Christian perspective, I believe it makes sense beyond a Christian context. In short, subbing out our charity and kindness to subcontractors allows us to feel good about what we are doing, but still allows us to remain in the same broken state that we now call home. Don't get me wrong. I am thankful for charities, shelters, etc., and donating to them is not a bad thing. Do not withhold your donations, just don't donate as a substitute for your own growth. I personally believe that politics and religion accomplish little to nothing, which is why I am not mentioning donations to them, and I believe your time, money, and energy would be much better spent with a local charity or shelter of some kind. Focusing on religion and government to create a society that I want to live in is in my opinion, the two places where you will spend the most of your energy, and get the least amount of results. They may be able to facilitate a changing society in some way, but not create or enact the change itself. I would even go as far as to say they are counterproductive when it comes to enacting true change. They in a way rely on things to stay the same. The one thinks change is evil, and both are afraid of what will happen when we no longer give them our focus. Society does have the ability to progress beyond both entities. I am working on all these things myself as I write this. I have by no means been the stellar example of all this, but am rather just coming into the realization or ideas of these things. My focus on becoming a better, happier, kinder person may be all I can handle at the moment, and may have a bigger impact than anything else can have.

So, if legislation and religions will not bring about the change that we all seek, and seem to hinder us instead, then what do we do? It can seem kind of pointless if the things that we have been taught are the most impactful in society, simply cannot deliver the results that we want. The things society finds unacceptable on a personal level and micro level, we need to apply to or cease to accept from our large systemic entities. We need government standards to catch up to personal standards. In large, it is no longer acceptable to shame, demonize, label, murder, etc., on personal level when you are out and about in the market, and yet our governments and religion still do this every day. This is once again the "god" complex that allows these systems to survive. They need the power to do great harm and evil in a way that no common person would find acceptable on a personal level. Most of the harm and hurt we see is being perpetuated by our systems, creating the pain and the trauma that causes people to act in a manner that is not true to themselves. We are in a sense, freely giving an otherwise nonexistent, synthetic system the very power it needs to survive. If we no longer give energy to these entities, they will die. They are not self-sustaining and only live as long as we give them life. Shift your focus and your energy away from manmade entities and focus your physical and spiritual energies elsewhere. Maybe, rather than looking to all the detached systems that have soaked up our energies, we need to be focused a little closer to home, more localized, maybe even within ourselves. The focus has always been "out there" in some government program or legislation. Our focus has always been on a distant divine being, just waiting to come and enact the change that this world needs. This once again brings in the analogy of attempting to hit a distant target by ricocheting a projectile off of another object. It will be way less accurate and carry far less energy than if it is directed straight from the source to the intended target. You can also view this as any substance that carries any energy such as electricity traveling through wires, water flowing through a pipe, or sound and light traveling through atmosphere. The more this energy is diverted, run through longer conduits, or gets bounced off of any reflector or anything that creates resistance, the less energy it contains when it reaches its intended destination, if it even gets there at all. Much energy will be dispersed and bled off uselessly way before its destination. In some cases, the energy can be completely depleted just attempting to reach its goal. I see energetic and well intentioned folks all around me focusing their energies on trying to enact change, in one way or the other, by bouncing their energies off of a third party such as politics, business, and religion. Most of the time these very kind and loving people seem to focus their energies on traditional systems that have been viewed as the most important places to change the world. Politics and its figures have been propped up to be extremely important in the preservation of freedom, peace, morality, economies, and the overall way of life that we wish to live. The same is true in our view of our religion, pushing to make our religion or denomination the dominant one so that the will of our deity can come to pass. The truth of it is that by focusing in these areas, we often overlook the change that we need to create within ourselves and in our local communities. Our local communities do not need more legislation or government run programs, but rather focused energy from their populace. By focusing on a political party or religious group, we are relying on one entity to create the change that takes a community of energetic individuals to accomplish. These political and religious systems and structures are just that, systems. They themselves have no power to do anything. They are just an extra, unnecessary gear in the machine, a cog in the wheel, that just serve to soak up extra energy without really accomplishing anything. We humans have focused on these same social systems and structures for thousands of years, but where has it gotten us? We are still stuck in many of the same repetitive cycles as the ancient cultures were. There have been technological advancements, but for things such as moral advancement, the way one person treats another, the way we view the world and the universe, have all come about through the evolution of society, through the development of our inner consciousness, despite government and religious influence.

Maybe the easiest way around these inhibitive social systems is to simply not participate. We have normally been taught that if you wish to eliminate something useless or evil that you must fight it and destroy it. This, however, just leads to more evil, violence and, destruction. It just repeats the cycle and gives way for the new movement to become something that needs to be fought by future generations. Any entity that relies on overpowering another through violence of action will someday be the evil entity that needs to be overthrown. If we do not like government and its officials soaking up our energy, then simply don't give it your energy. You are much bigger and much more powerful than any manmade system. These manmade systems may simply not be deserving of your time. Maybe if we do not prop up these systems, they will collapse on their own, with many evil actions and policies dying along with them, thereby bringing progress and healing in a more holistic way. Focus on yourself, your loved ones, and the community around you. Quit stressing about politics and the fight over religion. Don't give that your energy. You won't have any left for the things that really matter. Use that energy on yourself. Afterall, you can't really bring about change in society if you do not create that change within yourself first. I think that is why we subconsciously want things such as the local church or government to bring about the change that we want, because it requires little more than our tithe or vote, and requires little change or action on our part. That is also the very reason why it doesn't work. If you want a system to bring about change, but no one will change, then it is impossible for change to happen. Forcing a change upon a populace is just tyranny and does nothing to create true change within the hearts of a society. "A mind changed against its will is of the same opinion still" – I have no idea who said that first, but my wife said it a lot and it is very true.

Nobel Prize recipients Bohr and Heisenberg were great pioneers of quantum mechanics. I know this bunny trail goes along with some of the things mentioned previously, but they're so fascinating to me. Bohr theorized that light can either be a wave or a particle depending on how it is observed. He also observed and pioneered the idea of the quantum leap. This theory was observed in electrons, where they either absorb or emit the exact amount of energy necessary to instantaneously jump from one "track" to the other. Essentially these electrons were going from point A to point B without ever being between the two points. There was also the theory of quantum entanglement, where on particle could effect another particle that was otherwise completely separate and disconnected from each other. When one electron would change direction, it would cause another to do the same. If this works in such a tiny scale, could it work on a larger scale? What possibilities would be at our fingertips if we harnessed these capabilities? Maybe we do not need to develop the technology that can harness this energy. Maybe we just need to harness the idea of it, within ourselves. Could humanity as a collective come to realize how this quantum leap can happen, then use it from within ourselves somehow? This subject is a bit of a rabbit trail, but would it be possible? Would it help us to realize our true power? Maybe these things are already happening inside of us, and we just haven't manifested it yet. Maybe the advancement in technology won't be for us to discover or invent new machines and gadgets, but the advancement in realizing that we can manifest it ourselves, from within ourselves. Do I need a phone if I could communicate through an interconnectedness with others through an entanglement on a larger scale? Do I need a car, airplane, or rocket if I can take a quantum leap myself? Do we need production lines producing frivolous things if I can create my own reality? Maybe our evolution as a species isn't so much an advancement in brain size and function, but rather in the progressive realization of the things around us, the things available to us. Maybe our brain capacity grew because we came to realize new things, not the other way around. Maybe we are almost through the discovery of material things, and now need to dive into the things not seen, the non-material energies and possibilities. The field of exploration and invention remain wide open in other dimensions. Maybe it is a marriage of the two, which we are in the beginning stages of right now. I know this all may sound a bit wacky, but it may be as simple as collective society simply realizing that we can have more. We may collectively imagine a world with less pain and hurt and simply start moving in that direction. All it takes is a simple shift of focus from synthetic systems, to things more wholesome and life giving. A shift in focus, a moving of our energy is all it takes. If humanity would take this approach, I wholeheartedly believe that the progression of things would just happen naturally. It wouldn't be weird or crazy at all. Society would just simply advance in the direction it needs to go. Maybe, if the quantum leap on a grand scale is too much to think about, we could simply be able to harness the energy that is floating freely through the universe. Could we somehow capture this energy in our automobiles, airplanes, televisions, smart phones, vacuum cleaners, and so on, without the need of electric power plants. No,

I'm not talking about placing little solar panels on everything. I believe there are other ways to catch energy, and many more forms of energy to capture. Maybe we wouldn't need to plug in our cars if they could independently collect the energy out of the atmosphere around them. We can already wirelessly communicate across the globe, and charge devices without connecting wires to them. If radio waves can be sent and received wirelessly, could electricity or other forms of energy do the same thing? Maybe the energy doesn't need to be produced by us at all, maybe it is already available in abundance, just waiting to be harnessed.

Trauma and the impact it has is something that we all face in this life. The word trauma can be over used by some, and not given any credibility by others. Some will claim it anywhere they can, as if they thrive on it, while others will not acknowledge the effects of it in their lives at all. Neither approach is healthy. It can discredit people suffering through real trauma, and can cause society to flippantly wave off the word, or anyone using it, as yet another cliché. Seeing an actual therapist and talking about ones feelings are helpful and have brought great healing to many. I see a therapist from time to time and it truly is helpful. There seem to be two extreme camps when it comes to this as well. There are those that want to talk about their trauma to everyone any chance they get, and others who never talk about it. Once again, neither is healthy (in my unprofessional opinion). I do believe the healing of trauma goes way beyond talking about it, and we have overlooked, or lost touch with, some very helpful ways of dealing with trauma. I believe that we have lost touch with something our ancestors would have used extensively. I believe we have lost touch with ritual. Some may practice this to an extent in religious circles, however at large many of us simply do not participate in rituals on the deeper spiritual level of things. Ritual is a way of being able to recognize and feel trauma, pain, and fear in a healthy way. It gives you the ability to recognize it, pull it into reality, and then release it in a healthy way. I believe that the universe can absorb our negative or low vibrational energies in a healthy way. The forms of this negative energy that I believe will be mirrored back to us in an unhealthy way is when this negative energy comes out as violence, turmoil, subjugation, and hate towards others. However, when the anxiety that you feel in your chest is recognized, felt, and then released in a contemplative way, the universe can absorb it in much the same way that a tree can absorb CO_2 and produce oxygen with it. The creation around us truly can help us process through our emotions. The tightness in your chest, the heart palpitations, quite literally come from balls of energy stored up next to your heart or other organs. I believe this is why you can physically feal these things, because they are actual energies within yourself. I believe this is where a lot of heart problems and many health complications come from. Many are not willing to manifest this energy in a violent way (which is a good thing), but also lost touch with the ability to release it in a healthy ritualistic way. So it just sits there, eating away at you like a disease. I know to some religious people, the word "ritual" has some negative connotations around it. It doesn't mean a circle of people around a fire, dressed in dark hooded robes, chanting low rhythmic noises. It can simply be meditation, or it can be a person looking into ancient trauma healing and ritual and coming up with one that suites you best. Most of the time it does require a deep realization of the pain that is there and a visualization of the release of that pain. I believe this is why yoga and Buddhism have made a comeback, because they both practice deep meditation and a connectedness with one's emotions. Pain, fear, and anxiety seem to be emotions that, if avoided, seem to linger for as long as they are not recognized. Most of the time we avoid them because they scare us. We look at them as something negative. Normally they do not feel good, but are only there to let us know there are places that need healing in our lives. They're not bad. They only have negative consequences if not dealt with and left there to fester like an untreated wound. There is a big difference between pain from a cut, and the infection that sets in if left untreated. The pain is not bad, the infection is. Ignore the pain of a cut and leave it untreated, infection will invariably set in. Sure, sometimes the act of cleaning and bandaging a wound can in itself create pain, but not near as much as the infection could. Much of the pain and anxiety I faced in my life surprisingly went away very quickly once I actually took the time to look at them, bring them into existence and gave them the time they needed. What looked like this huge wall that would take so much work to bring down, I could normally walk through very quickly and easily. I also realized that after giving it the space it required, I could normally release it in a healthy way. I could send it away, not in a hateful way, but more like waving goodbye to a friend. I know this may sound magical, but it's not. Pain and trauma will remain there until dealt with. Pain and trauma will build up like compounding interest on a debt, and will only go away if dealt with in a real way. Ritual will help you in this. Going out in bare feet and grounding with the earth can draw some of these out, or re-energize you like charging a battery. Trauma and negative energy can be released out into the universe, and it will gladly take it from you and turn it into something lifegiving.

I know that the above paragraph sounds a little "rainbow and butterflies". I realize that not all trauma and pain are dealt with only in this "sit with it and release it" way. Some of the serious things we endure really do take a lot of painful work. Some of this stuff does need to be given time, and periods of emotional pain are necessary. Many different approaches can be taken. Talking to friends and therapists are definitely necessary. I do believe that the practice of ritual can still be a powerful tool to use in this endeavor of healing. I also think many people have hobbies and such that they call their therapy. Most of the time these hobbies and activities are used more as a distraction to forget the underlying pain. Take the constant activity away, and all the pain and trauma bubble to the surface again. Real therapy will help you engage the pain, not avoid it. I know people who cannot sit still, be alone, or take silence. We rely on busyness and constant noise to distract us from our real emotions. The constant need for sports, cars, camping, etc., may (not always) be more of a need to avoid your internal state, rather than a healthy activity springing forth out of happiness. I also believe that ritual can help us keep a healthy emotional immune system. It can keep small cuts from becoming gangrenous through the constant awareness of our inner selves. Before modern medicine, there was no real understanding of germs and their effects. Small scrapes and cuts could develop infections that could result in the loss of a limb, or even cause death. Very minor steps of cleanliness and care that we take for granted today, were often overlooked as a none-necessity, thereby leading to infections of all kinds. I believe the same is true in our emotional and spiritual health. If we do not know the cause and effects of our emotional and spiritual wellbeing, then seemingly small offenses can lead to trauma if left untreated.

I also believe that ignoring our internal state can very much lead to physical ailments, disease, and a breakdown of our physical immune system. I do not believe we connect our emotional and spiritual health with our physical health nearly as much as we should. We seem to focus on the things we can feal, see, taste, and touch, not realizing that the non-material things are every bit as real and powerful. Engaging in some form of ritual can not only bring you back to center, but also bring healing to small hurts before they develop into something much bigger. Call it preventative maintenance for the soul if you like.

Change yourself. It quite literally is all you can do, and it is way more powerful than you may think. In changing yourself, you will ultimately go out and radiate that change into the society around you. This may be through your willingness to help others, the smile on your face, or the energy that is radiating out from you. All of these things are energy (or require it) and will positively impact whatever space you occupy. Furthermore, I perceive goodness and kindness as being similar to the theory of light as being both a wave and a particle, depending on our observation of it. You can test it as a wave or as a particle and it will act according to how it is tested. You could almost say that you can create it into whichever state that you choose to observe it in. The idea that light energy can travel as a wave, very much unhindered by empty space, yet materialize as (or at least act like) a particle when observed is so awesome. I believe it goes beyond light. It is almost as if there is hidden energy out there that cannot materialize until we begin to look for it. It is almost as if we pull things, possibilities, and potentials, from around us into existence as a tangible thing, upon our recognition of it. Things around us could also change from one thing into another depending on how we choose to see them. Our focus may be able to change evil into good, depending on what energy you give it, or how you choose to observe it. The same energy given towards something evil can also be given towards something good. If there is a mirror in the universe that reflects or manifests disease and inclement weather, etc., from our negative energies that we project from ourselves, could humanity's focused energy either mitigate or transform those evils into something wholesome and good, depending on how we choose to view them? Do we give life to whatever things we focus on? Could we feed this universe a more positive energy, thus giving it the ability to mirror it back to us, replacing disease and famine with health and vitality? Could it be that the only thing that is needed to heal our planet, to heal humanity, is for me to heal myself?